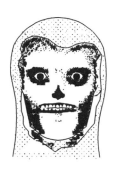

HAUNTED HOUSE HALLOWEEN HANDBOOK

Haunted House Halloween Handbook

by

JERRY CHAVEZ

McFarland & Company, Inc., Publishers
Jefferson, North Carolina, and London

Special thanks to Nancy Hubbs Chang and Maureen A. Williamson.
This book could not have been completed without their help and suggestions.
I would also like to thank all the authors of all the other books I have ever read.
And finally I would like to thank my parents for everything else.

Notice: This book is presented only as a means of preserving a heritage of theatrical arts. Author and publisher make no representation, warranty or guarantee that the techniques or information described or illustrated in this book will be safe for the reader, the haunted house designer-producer or its clientele or visitors in any situation or under any conditions. Author and publisher accept no responsibility for any injury resulting from the application of any technique described or illustrated in this book.

British Library Cataloguing-in-Publication data are available

Library of Congress Cataloguing-in-Publication Data

Chavez, Jerry.
Haunted house Halloween handbook / by Jerry Chavez.
p.   cm.
Includes index.
ISBN 0-7864-0375-6 (sewn softcover : 55# alkaline paper) ∞
1. Halloween decorations.   2. Haunted houses.   I. Title.
TT900.H32C48   1997
745.594'1— DC21
97-23721   CIP

Manufactured in the United States of America

McFarland & Company, Inc., Publishers
Box 611, Jefferson, North Carolina 28640

To Samantha Suzana Swint.
I still love you
wherever you are.

Contents

Preface

"Go on, kids," their mother said, pointing to my front door. It was a perfect Halloween night. The moon was full, and there were a few clouds but no rain. I had spent the whole week after school getting ready for this. At 12 I felt too old to go trick-or-treating, and this was more fun!

For most of my youth I lived on a small island in the Pacific ("Guam, where America's day begins"). There was nothing to do but read books. I read books on magic tricks and how magicians perform mock seances. I read about makeup artists and toy making. I got very good at creating my own toys. I tore apart clocks and other gadgets just to see how they worked. By the time I began designing spooky effects for Halloween, I had learned a great deal and become very resourceful.

My two young victims left the safety of their mom. "Go get the candy, and remember to say thank-you," she called. The two children slowly walked up my driveway, past the creepy eyes that glowed from the bushes. As they approached, I turned on the recording of a barking dog and shook the branches with a yank of a string. The poor kids looked back to their mother, who waved encouragingly.

With noticeable reluctance, the little boy led his sister up to my "haunted porch" and knocked on the door. Eerie music and the wail of demons oozed from the windows of my living room. The door seemed to open by itself. A small TV tray, draped with a white tablecloth and holding a bowl of candy, slowly rose from the floor and bobbed across the room to the doorway. It passed through the doorway out to the screaming children.

They turned to run away, but before they could make it to their mother, spiders dropped from the ceiling of the front porch. One swung down, blocking the exit, then just as quickly popped back up. The children's mother, laughing a little, came up to get the candy for them.

I spent the day after Halloween cleaning up the trick effects and eating leftover candy. As usual, I had a lot of candy left over.

To atone for the sins of my childhood, I now design haunted houses for charitable organizations. These attractions can be very profitable for any group willing to put the work into a good presentation. Depending on the scope of the project, the profits can range from a few hundred to many thousands of dollars.

A group planning a haunted house faces many challenges. Will the location be adequate? Will it meet safety regulations? Will the volunteers work effectively? Will the budget be adequate? Most important, will the customers be scared? Will the effects produce delicious shivers, derisive laughter, or yawns?

In twenty years of designing haunted houses, I have learned a lot about all these challenges and more. I hope now to share what I have learned with the readers of this book. I have attempted to provide information on every aspect of haunted house operation, including location, design, safety, props, illusions, makeup, costumes, advertising, and showmanship.

There are tips on working within a budget, qualifying for legal permits, using sound and light effects, building illusions, and obtaining unusual supplies. With this book, any reader should find the help he or she needs to pull off a project of any size, from a small "haunted porch" to a full-scale attraction with sophisticated illusions and professional-style special effects.

In short, it has been my goal to write the kind of book I looked for (in vain) when I was an aspiring haunter. I hope I have succeeded, and that many happy hauntings will arise from these pages. Good luck!

Very ghouly yours,
Jerry R. Chavez

1. Getting Started

Start-Up Costs and Sponsorship

Most of the time a haunted house is sponsored by an organization that will have access to start-up capital. Before you draw up your budget, read all the way through this book to get an idea of the expenses involved. Next, make a list of the expenses you will incur (see the form on the following page).

Always overestimate! Surprises can be expensive. I once had $1000 worth of lumber delivered to a haunted house site. Because it was donated, I could not really dictate when it would be dropped off. Overnight more than half of the studs and panels were stolen from the backyard of the building. I had to cover the expense with my overestimation fund. It could have been a disaster.

The average first-rate charity fundraiser haunted house will cost approximately $1.55 per square foot, just for materials. However, creativity can greatly reduce start-up costs. I have never been involved with a haunted house that lost money, largely because donated materials and man-hours keep costs low.

If you develop a good business plan, your organization might obtain money and materials from various businesses in the community in exchange for the publicity. (You can give credit to these sponsors in your ads, or list them on a printed program that you distribute to haunted house customers.)

Accounting

On the next page you will find a form entitled "Projected Expenses." This form will help you estimate the costs involved in building and operating your haunted house. Following the expense projection form is a "Project Record Sheet," designed to force you to think about every aspect of each prop or set you intend to build. It will also help you to communicate your ideas to your builders and sponsors.

A third form, "Supplies Accounting," will help you keep track of the actual cost of your supplies as you go along. Always keep good expense records. They will be valuable for IRS audits and will give you much information for future haunted house projects.

Workforce

Make a list of all the people that will be needed to operate the house: builders and

PROJECTED EXPENSES

	$ COST
BOOKKEEPING AND ACCOUNTING	
LOCATION	
UTILITIES	
PLANS AND CONSTRUCTION DRAWINGS	
BUILDING PERMIT	
FIRE PREVENTION (EXTINGUISHERS, FIRE RETARDANT)	
FIRE MARSHAL'S APPROVAL PERMIT	
BUSINESS PERMIT	
WALL MATERIALS	
WALL CONSTRUCTION LABOR	
INSURANCE (BASIC LIABILITY)	
DECORATIONS	
PROPS AND ILLUSIONS, SOUND SYSTEM	
ADVERTISING	
ACTORS AND OPERATORS	
COSTUMES AND MAKEUP	
UNIFORMED SECURITY PERSONNEL.	
MISCELLANEOUS EXPENSES.	
TOTAL EXPENSES	

ADVERTISING DOLLARS × 1 = NUMBER OF CUSTOMERS EXPECTED (LARGE OPERATION)
ADVERTISING DOLLARS × 4 = NUMBER OF CUSTOMERS EXPECTED (SMALL OPERATION)
NUMBER OF CUSTOMERS DIVIDED BY 150* = NUMBER OF HOURS TO OPERATE

*Based on the estimation that 150 customers can be moved through the entrance in one hour. You may need to revise this figure based on your haunted house's capacity.

PROJECT RECORD SHEET

PROJECT NAME _____ DATE _____

DESCRIPTION _____

FRONT VIEW

SIDE VIEW

ISOMETRIC VIEW

NOTES _____

BASIC MATERIALS (QTY)   COST

_____

TOTAL _____

SUPPLIES ACCOUNTING

DATE: _____

SHEET _____

NOTE	RECEIPT #	ITEM	COST	BUDGET BALANCE
TOTALS				

NOTES

☐ ☐ ☐ ☐ ☐ ☐ ☐ ☐ ☐ ☐

maintenance people, performers, security personnel and group escorts, and clerical and advertising people. If you are using volunteers, you cannot expect to have all your help all the time. One way around this problem is to hire your workers, but doing so will drive up your expenses, and you may have to conform to labor laws regarding taxation and insurance.

A better answer is to prepay your volunteers' gas expenses (a token set amount of perhaps $20 each) and bind them to a contract to make sure they will be where they should be, when they should be, doing what they should be doing.

Recruit people who are dependable and motivated. Make sure they understand that this will be a fun but demanding project. Key performing positions may best be done by aspiring actors; look to local drama schools or college drama departments. Nothing spoils a beautiful stage or a clever illusion more than a bad actor!

Security is more important than most haunted house organizers think. You should have one professional or off-duty police officer standing near the ticket booth. An escort equipped with a flashlight should *follow*, not lead, each group of customers through the house.

Be sure that these escorts are mature and can handle unruly customers by their presence. You don't really want macho bouncers; look for the strong, silent type. Tall or uniformed individuals will have a command presence that may deter problems. The escorts are for safety and should never speak or turn on their flashlights unless absolutely necessary!

Hold regular meetings for staff communication. Use the handout on the next page to remind workers of the rules, and have everyone show up *early* for the performances.

Location

Next to advertising, this is the most important consideration, and often the most problematical because it involves customer satisfaction, a big chunk of the budget, and the wonderful world of government red tape. You might think that an old Victorian house would be perfect — but think again. The floor plans of the average house are not only inconvenient for traffic flow, but rarely conform to the local authorities' idea of a "safe amusement building."

When selecting a location think about parking, accessibility to major roads, and the size of the haunted house you can afford to run. The best locations for this kind of haunted house tend to be slots in an open air shopping mall. If you can get the space donated for 30 days you may still need to pay for the electricity and water. I have also seen giant tents (3600 square feet) built in parking lots with electricity brought in or a gas generator used. You will need about 0.017 amps of electricity per square foot.

If a giant tent is used, make sure that the tent has a state fire marshal stamp on it to certify that it is fireproof. The company that rents you this tent is responsible for this stamp, but make sure it is where it can be seen.

Make sure that the building can be locked up, or at least have a night watchman for the off hours. Haunted houses and Halloween can bring out all sorts of curious people.

Depending on the scope of your project, you may have to conform to the strict fire codes for "amusement buildings." This term was recently created to cover haunted houses. Go to your local library to find fire codes for your area. The book you will be looking for will have a title along the lines of *[State's name] Life Safety Code Handbook*.

HAUNTED HOUSE OPERATORS HANDOUT

WHEN

_____
_____
_____
_____

WHERE

In the "Green Room,"
Rear Entrance;
Sign in at the Door

WHAT TO BRING

Folding Chair
Black Clothing and Dark Shoes
  or Assigned Costume
Flashlight with Fresh Batteries
32-Ounce Bottle of Water with Your Name on It

1 DO NOT USE FLASHLIGHTS UNLESS ABSOLUTELY NECESSARY.

2 DO NOT ALLOW GROUPS OF MORE THAN 6 PEOPLE TO ENTER AT A TIME.

3 WALK BEHIND THE GROUP AS AN ESCORT, NOT IN FRONT AS A LEADER.

4 DO NOT ALLOW PUSHING.

5 DO NOT ALLOW FOOD OR DRINKS.

6 DO NOT ALLOW FLASH PHOTOGRAPHY.

7 DO NOT TOUCH CUSTOMERS UNLESS ABSOLUTELY NECESSARY.

8 DO NOT TALK TO CUSTOMERS INSIDE THE HOUSE UNLESS ABSOLUTELY NECESSARY.

9 DO NOT TOUCH ANY PROPS OR ILLUSIONS.

10 DO NOT ALLOW CUSTOMERS TO TOUCH ANY PROPS OR ILLUSIONS.

11 DO NOT EXPLORE ANY PART OF THE HOUSE THAT CUSTOMERS CANNOT EXPLORE.
   (DO NOT WANDER INTO THE BACKSTAGE AREAS.)

12 DO NOT TRY TO ADJUST OR REPAIR ANY FAILED DEVICE. REPORT IT TO MAINTENANCE.

13 PASSAGE THROUGH THE HOUSE IS ONE WAY ONLY, FROM THE ENTRANCE TO THE EXIT.

14 WHEN THE HOUSE CLOSES FOR THE NIGHT MEET IN THE GREEN ROOM BEFORE LEAVING.

You will need to read the information on "assembly occupancies" and special provisions for "amusement buildings." For more on safety considerations, see "Legal and Safety Considerations" immediately below.

If you can obtain a shopping mall slot, many safety requirements are satisfied and you have the benefit of an overhead sprinkler system.

Legal and Safety Considerations

Usually, local officials are understanding when dealing with a charity, but you must make every effort to comply with all fire and safety regulations. Have the fire department inspect your ideas and offer you suggestions on the safety aspect of your floor plans and special effects before starting construction. You will need to start the fire marshal's paperwork several weeks before opening the haunted house anyway.

If you have a lawyer or construction contractor involved with your charity, consult that person. If not, perhaps someone will donate his or her services.

Some areas of concern with safety and law are:

• Safety ordinances (fire, structural, electrical, sanitation, OSHA requirements)

• Licenses for operation (occupational permits; state, local, and county business permits)

• Zoning (area use permits)

• Labor (workman's compensation, minimum wage, and tax withholding)

• Liability (insurance in case someone is injured)

The easiest way to take care of all these problems is to hire licensed contractors and lawyers to protect your interests, but this would probably break your budget. Try to find donated expertise. Remember that some of these regulations may be legally waived for nonprofit groups.

You may be forced by the fire marshal to buy liability insurance. Why the fire marshal is the one to enforce this I have no idea. All I can tell you is that sometimes the paperwork to get a fire inspection requires your insurance number and carrier.

The average cost of insurance is about $100 a day for each day you are serving customers. A more practical way to get insurance is to buy a rider to the insurance that your club already carries. Sometimes the insurance you presently carry will cover the haunted house. Most colleges and schools already have insurance for "special events" (as the insurance company calls them).

The insurance company will want to know about how many people you expect to buy tickets, where the event will be held, how much you will charge, and how many days the event will last. It is a good idea to tell them about all the precautions you have, such as emergency exits, fire extinguishers, fire alarms, water sprinkler systems, etc.

Be as friendly and cooperative as possible with the local fire marshal who will inspect your haunted house. He or she has the authority to waive some of the regulations, but the fire marshal is responsible for having waived these regulations if a fire breaks out. If the marshal feels that you are doing your best and operating safely, you should pass the inspection. But if he wants to, he can close you down on the smallest technicality!

In my opinion this is very unfair. A house that has passed one marshal's inspection may be closed down by a different marshal just because that marshal is having a bad day. Most of the time officials really will try hard to work with you, but you have no practical recourse if the fire marshal will not okay your project. It's up to his or her individual interpretation of the law.

Local fire codes are adopted from "recommendations" made by a group called the N.F.P.A. (National Fire Prevention Association). To be in the N.F.P.A. you must pay fees. The industries that are greatly affected by fire regulations pay a great deal to put their own people in this "association." This way they can influence what the rules will be and they will know what to be prepared for so they can get a jump on the competition.

That makes N.F.P.A. officials non-elected law makers, and their self-regulating leaves much to be desired. Because the average person does not organize public functions, few people are aware of the most cumbersome regulations, which consequently go unchallenged.

Most states have a sales tax on all purchases. There are even amusement taxes in some areas. Most states require an organization to register with its tax office. Many states offer non-profit groups a tax exemption. This means that you do not have to pay taxes on your products. Your group probably has a tax number. If not, call the nearest state office building and you will get a number or the information for filing.

Here is a list of safety suggestions:

• Most of the time your house will be required to have emergency exits that swing out from the building. These exits will need to be about 50 feet from each other. Special doors should be built if customers will be deep inside a maze of walls. These doors will be decorated to match the walls but should have emergency exit signs on them. This way, if an alarm occurs, the escorts and the actors can quickly take the customers out of the middle of the "house."

Always design the doors to be *pushed, not pulled open*. Use a screen door spring to hold them in place. The state life safety codes handbook will have specific information. The corridors will need to be at least four feet wide, and very low ceilings that require the customers to crawl are normally illegal.

• Use a panic light system. Panic lights operate on battery power. In the event that the regular lights fail, the panic lights automatically come on. Your group should find out if these lights are required.

Most codes also require the ability to quickly turn on overhead lighting and shut off any confusing sounds or illusions in case of an emergency. This could be done by large electric relays or a person standing ready at the circuit switches. Communication is important for smooth operation as well as emergencies. You might consider renting high quality walkie-talkies or hand-held CB units.

• Even if you have panic lights, be sure everyone on the staff has flashlights, but stress that no one is to turn on a flashlight unless it is important. Stray light beams can ruin effects and temporarily blind customers, making the haunted house a dangerous environment. *Flash photography* should not be allowed for the same reason. Do not allow customers to enter with cameras.

• Have your own "safety marshal." Assign this job to one person, and have him or her make regular inspections.

• Do not allow smoking in the house. Strictly enforce this rule. Expel anyone violating it. It is absolutely illegal and dangerous to let anyone smoke in the haunted house. The fire marshal will require you to have signs up to enforce this regulation.

• Do not allow open fires, smoke pots or hot effects in the house. It is very easy to create a flame effect with lights, fans and scrim cloth (see page 45).

• Have a closing checklist and cut off all power to lights, fans, motors and so forth.

• There are basically three types of fire extinguishers. The soda style is for use on burning wood, paper and cloth. The CO^2 style is used on electrical fires. You should use the third kind, which puts out both fire types. Ask a hardware store to donate the extinguishers. You probably won't use them and will be able to return them. The fire marshal will require that extinguishers be recently serviced by a licensed company.

• Have regular fire drills. Practice with staff members. Make sure all escorts know the exits.

• Separate the audience from the actors and scenes by using rails, fences, and half-partitions. These will prevent people from wandering into the scenes. I like to paint the rails black and cover them with cobwebs to make a fence that does not look out of place in a haunted house (always strive for theme and continuity).

• Keep a first-aid kit handy. If possible, have someone trained in first aid or a volunteer nurse on duty. Having an EMT (emergency medical technician) is preferable.

• If your house has stairs, illuminate them. You must make stairs visible.

• Have a telephone in the office with all the emergency numbers posted (fire, police, hospital).

• Painting your walls with fire-retardant paint should fulfill the fire code requirements for fireproofing the walls. If you use drywall, you won't have to worry about fireproofing. Drywall is a pressed sheet of plasterlike material. (You may have heard it

called "Sheetrock." This is a brand name.) You can get drywall from any home improvement center.

• For props, try to use materials that will not burn. Instructions on flameproofing are available from the library or fire station. If you should end up with materials that have not been treated, you may have to treat them yourself.

Listed below are two formulas. All you have to do is mix one of these formulas and spray it on your props. It is important that you still test the flammability of your props after they have been treated and thoroughly dried. The object tested may catch on fire, but the flames should quickly die out.

The first formula:

> 1 pound Borax
> 1 pound sal ammoniac (ammonium chloride)

Dissolve in 3 quarts water. Add a few ounces of acetic acid or 20 ounces of vinegar to help counteract the corrosive effect of this spray on metals.

The second formula:

> Dissolve 10 pounds ammonium sulfamate (made by DuPont) into 5 gallons warm water.

Try Dixco chemicals in Anaheim, Calif., (714) 535-0646, or check your local phone book for a chemical distributor. Local theatrical supply companies will have "approved" and premixed formulas, but they are likely to be expensive.

If the fire codes are very strict, you may have to have a licensed company fireproof your materials. Again this requirement may be waived if you demonstrate every effort to adhere to or exceed the other safety precautions. Normally the fire marshal will be concerned only with large cloth or paper items (curtains and large papier-mâché props).

To make spider webs, buy material called "Stretchy Spider Webs." The material is very inexpensive and can be taken down and used again and again. *Read the package to see if it is fireproof.* Some theater supply companies will rent out a "web maker" that sprays a chemical web. I do not suggest you use this as most of the formulas used are very flammable. (A non-flammable formula can be bought from Terror by Design, 632 Oriole Drive, Streamwood, IL 60107; phone: (630) 830-9561; Fax (630) 830-9577.)

The primary concern in fire control is not *whether* it will burn, but *how long* it will burn until the fire can pass through and spread to the rest of the haunted house. Focus your efforts on the assumption that something *will* catch on fire and that your precautions are to stop the fire from spreading.

2. Layout and Construction

Floor Plans

You will be required to submit the floor plans of your haunted house to the city fire marshal and the city planner if you plan to obtain permits for operation. If possible, obtain the basic floor plans of the building that you will be constructing your haunted house in. If you've rented a slot at a mall, you can obtain these from the management. You'll need several copies of the plans in order to work out ideas.

If you can't obtain the basic floor plans, you'll have to measure the space yourself and draw it to the best of your ability. These plans must be done with drafting tools. The straight-edged triangle and compass will be your most important tools.

The better the drawings, the more likely it is that inspectors will pass your plans. It sounds crazy, but the better looking the plans, the more positive the inspector's attitude will be. It makes the inspectors feel that you know what you are doing when the plan and the work look neat and tidy. Getting help from a draftsman, architect, building contractor, or carpenter will greatly simplify the drawing process.

If you have access to a computer and drawing software, you may be able to submit 11" × 8½" drawings to the inspectors. If your haunted house is very large, you will not be able to get away with this. You could draw the plans on a computer in a 30" × 42" format (this is known as C size). Print them out in sections, tape them together and then have the taped original copied with a large-format copy machine.

Well-equipped copy shops sometimes have these machines; if you can't find one, try your local phone book for "drafting services." These services will have large copy machines but probably will charge you between $5 and $20 per copy.

Normally you will need one copy for yourself, which will be stamp-approved by the building inspector's office, and one that the inspector may want to keep. Since you are building a temporary structure, however, the inspector may not need to keep a copy.

You will need to show the walls, internal doors, exit doors or openings, fire extinguisher placement, heat detector placement and dimensions of the space from one wall to the other.

Use arrows and dotted lines to show the flow of traffic. You must draw anything that could get in the way of the customer's escape path in case of an emergency.

Any symbols used should be identified on the drawings in a key. Don't forget a scale if your drawing is to scale.

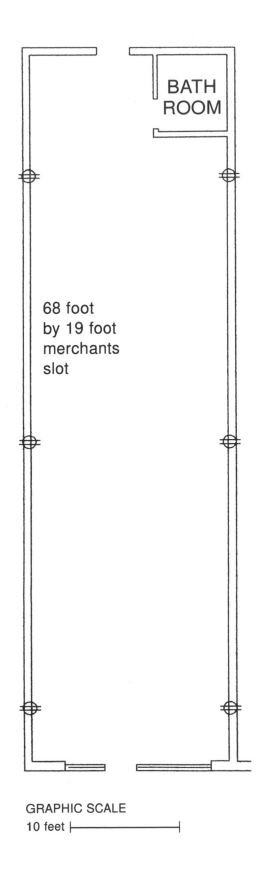

BATH
ROOM

68 foot
by 19 foot
merchants
slot

GRAPHIC SCALE

10 feet

HIGHLAND PLAZA HAUNTED HOUSE

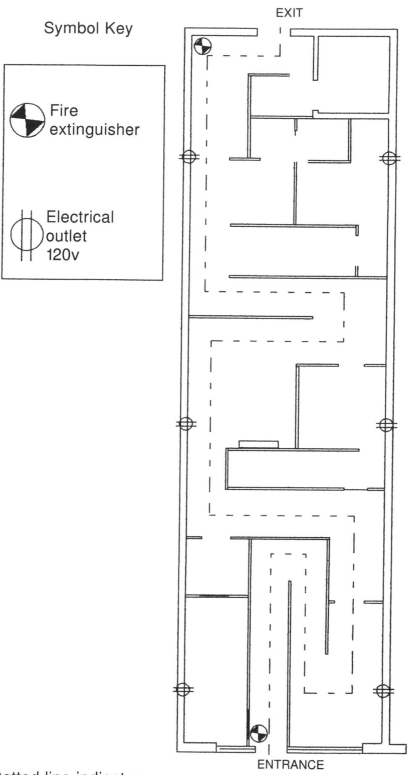

Symbol Key

Fire extinguisher

Electrical outlet 120v

EXIT

ENTRANCE

Dotted line indicates the customer's egress.

Now you will need a set of floor plans that the special effects crew will use. Using these floor plans, pencil in where your effects and "boos" (startling occurrences) will be. Also draw in symbols for the lights, extension cords with power strips, sound effects/speakers, electrical outlets, and operators/actors.

Your floor plans should be developed around your performance. Give your utmost attention to the timing and placement of your effects. In any good show, the first effect should be quick and dazzling to grab the customers' interest, and the last effect should be the best and strongest. Keep the level of excitement building to a grand finale.

For more about effective presentations, I suggest acquiring *Magic and Showmanship* by Henning Nelms (Dover Publications, Inc., New York, 1969). This excellent book will give you much insight into showmanship and the presentation of illusions.

The customers' interest in your show will not remain constant. If you do not increase it, it will slump. The customers are entertained only while interest is rising. When the interest slacks off, the spectators relax. If a drop in interest continues for more than a few seconds, they become bored. Your success depends on your ability to make interest rise for the maximum length of time and fall for the minimum length of time.

Try not to let your customers' interest peak prematurely. You will create a false climax that will make everything that occurs later seem weak by comparison. Each peak

---

Key to floor plan on opposite page:

1 ENTRANCE
2 GIRL CHANGE
3 SPIDERS/BAT/SNAKE
4 DOLL ROOM
5 ZOMBIE DINNER
6 FIRE IN FIREPLACE
7 FLOATING FURNITURE
8 HAND THROUGH WALL
9 MIRROR GHOST
10 PEPPER'S GHOST

Ⓢ SOUND EFFECTS LIST	TAPE TYPE	TAPE TIME
1 THEME MUSIC	LOOP	3 MINUTES
2 DEMON SCREAM	LOOP	20 SECONDS
3 DOLL LAUGHTER	LOOP	20 SECONDS
4 LIGHTNING	LOOP	20 SECONDS
5 HEART POUNDING	LOOP	20 SECONDS
6 THEME MUSIC	LOOP	3 MINUTES
7 CLOCK GONG	LOOP	20 SECONDS
8 TRAPPED SPIRIT	LOOP	20 SECONDS
9 THEME MUSIC	LOOP	3 MINUTES

NOTE: SPEAKER 6 AND 9 ARE CONNECTED TO THE SAME PLAYER.

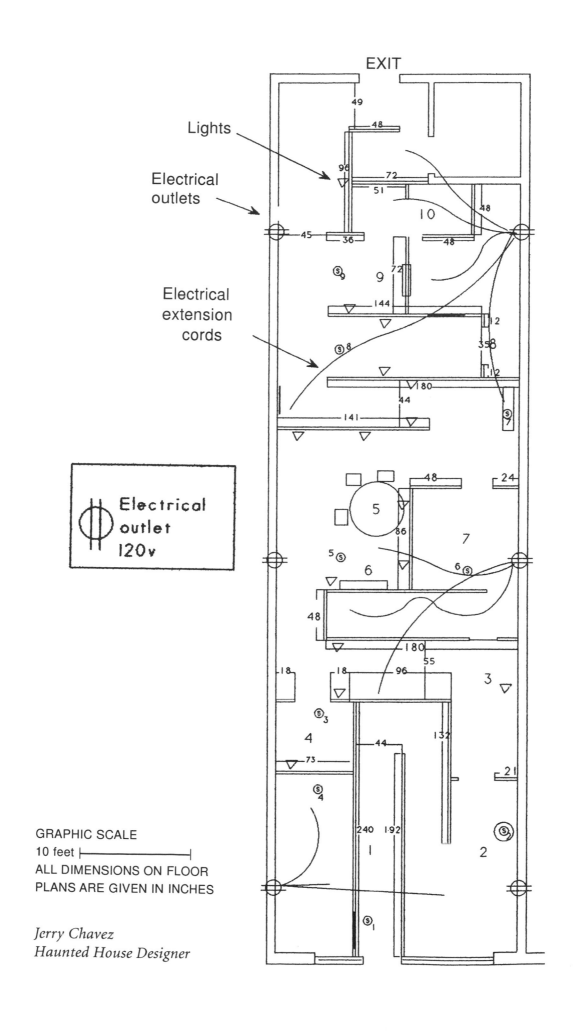

EXIT

Lights

Electrical outlets

Electrical extension cords

Electrical outlet 120v

GRAPHIC SCALE
10 feet
ALL DIMENSIONS ON FLOOR
PLANS ARE GIVEN IN INCHES

Jerry Chavez
Haunted House Designer

of interest should be higher than the one before it. Keep your customers in place only long enough for the maximum effect, then slowly move them along to the next point of interest.

The techniques for creating rising interest are a basic part of showmanship. They will do more to earn customer satisfaction than all the blood and chainsaws of all the other haunted houses put together.

You should draw a "storyboard" of your haunted house and each room or effect to help you plan and visualize the performance. A storyboard is a set of simple drawings that depict the show from the customer's point of view.

And speaking of point of view, be aware that most illusions must have a controlled "line of sight." The line of sight is the trajectory of an imaginary line that could be drawn from the illusion to the customer's eyes. Any possible angle and direction that the customer might use to see an effect should be tested. You must put yourself in the position of a curious and perhaps impolite customer who will use every angle to look at your effect in order to figure out how you are doing it.

By the way, as an entertainer, you must realize it is unethical to go around telling people how the effects and illusions are accomplished. You will find that most people are actually *disappointed* when they find out how "simple" the illusion is. As laypersons they cannot appreciate the subtle complexities and artistic effort. Some people even feel stupid (because the secret seems so simple), which puts them into a negative frame of mind.

So anyone who does not need to know how the effect works (including escorts in some cases) should not be told. The standard response from most magicians to how-does-it-work questions is, "It's done with mirrors." Another response is to ask the inquirer, "Can you keep a secret even if your best friend wants to know?" When the inquirer replies, "Sure I can," you answer, "So can I!" Or simply tell them it is a trade secret, which is the truth.

Your staff of escorts should understand this also. Often customers will ask their escorts how this or that is done. Train them to reply, "I don't know, I just work here."

Returning to the subject of layout, another element you must consider is *egress*, the flow of the crowd from entrance to exit. Keep all egress going in a one-way direction. Try not to have the crowd flow cross over itself. That could cause confusion. Basically, keep customers moving along one direction at all times (no doubling back). Remember to keep your corridors four feet wide whenever possible.

Emergency or "chicken" exits should be spaced 30 to 60 feet away from each other with the doors opening to the outside. This prevents a crowd from pushing up against closed doors and trapping themselves inside. Provide concealed doors or passages for the haunted house operators to quickly move through the house without disturbing customers.

Use duct tape and aluminum foil to cover the inside of all windows to block out any light. Complete control of light inside your haunted house is vital.

Keep aware of "startle zones." These are places where the customers will become suddenly excited and may jump into the wall opposite the effect that startled them. The wall they will back into must be built with extra support.

It is best to try to use the existing walls of the building your house will be constructed in. Otherwise, make sure the wall the customers will hit is *very* strong! Test it by having three adults run into it.

You will need to buy exit signs with arrows pointing the way out. These will need to be placed every 30 to 60 feet away from each other. Check your local fire marshal codes for the exact specifications of these exit signs. Strict codes require certain colors and letter heights.

It may be possible to adhere to those requirements with signs that can be duplicated on white paper and have them photocopied with red ink, which will greatly reduce the cost. Signs can be bought at hardware stores but range from $5 to $10 apiece.

Exit signs must be placed at a certain height, approximately seven feet from the floor, but you should check the exact fire codes for your area. Some codes will require exit signs a foot off the floor also. This is in case thick smoke from a fire forces customers to crawl on the floor.

Never have operators or escorts walk opposite the crowd flow. Have them go around to the front of the house. You may want to set aside one isolated room for costume changes and makeup. In the theater, this is called the "green room" and is used for actors' breaks or meetings. If possible, the green room should be next to the bathroom.

All stairs should be well lit. I don't build any stairs in my haunted houses; I use a 30-degree ramp instead. Treat the surface of the ramp to prevent slipping. Use rubber mats or put sand in the final coat of paint. This will avoid structural-permit problems and make the house more wheelchair accessible.

(Note: Because a haunted house is not a "public accommodation" like a restaurant, hotel, or retail store, handicapped access is not mandated, but of course it is in your best interest to make the house accessible to all comers.)

Basic Construction Tools

The following tools will be particularly useful in the initial construction of your haunted house. Most of these tools you may already have access to. Some you will be able to rent.

Adjustable wrench: The 10-inch wrench will work for most jobs.

Angle vise: This special carpenter's vise holds wood studs at a 45-degree angle to each other, making for fast and easy frame construction. These come in two sizes, one for 2" × 4" studs and one for smaller studs such as 1" × 2" studs.

Awl: Used to punch or dent material in preparation for drilling. This eliminates the "walking" or "drifting" of a drill bit.

Belt sander: Use a belt sander for smoothing and shaping a variety of materials (wood, hard foam, plastic, fiberglass, even soft metals). It can be turned upside down and C-clamped to a work bench. Tape the trigger in the ON position and you have yourself a bench sander. This way you can use both hands to hold and turn the subject being sanded.

C-clamps: A set of two 5" clamps is the minimum you'll need. More is better — much better.

Carpenter's square: Lays out long lines for such jobs as stair stringers and wall bracing.

Chalkline: Marks long lines more accurately than just a pencil and square.

Combination square: Lays out cutting lines and checks board square and joint alignment.

Drywall screw: A special long screw usually used to fasten drywall to steel beams. Use it to fasten wood together; it is better than using nails because it can be screwed in and out quickly with a drill and a special attachment.

One drawback is that it tends to split wood if you do not drill a hole first, but with two drills (one to drill a hole and one to shoot the drywall screw in) it is still faster and more versatile than nailing.

Another trick is to dip the drywall screw into a lubricant such as car wax. This will reduce the resistance and allow the screw to penetrate the wood much more easily. Be careful, though, because two studs that are being screwed together this way may drift apart in the process. If this happens, just back out the screw and redrive it into the wood. This will give you a very tight bond. Drywall screws are available at hardware stores.

Electric drill: Get a variable speed, reversible ⅜" drill with twist and spade bit sets. If you will be drilling into masonry materials such as concrete floors, you may need a "hammer drill." This is a special drill that uses masonry bits with a bouncing action to chisel its way through concrete or brick.

Four-in-hand: This is a combination tool with a half-round rasp and file.

Hammer: You'll need a 16-ounce, forged steel head with a smooth bell face. You may also need a ball peen hammer to set percussion rivets for leather work and metal fastening.

The rivet is placed against a hard heavy support such as an anvil. Then the rivet is flattened a little to make it wider. Finally it is struck with the ball side of the hammer to smash the head of the rivet into a mushroom shape. This is done by striking off cen-

ter so that the ball head of the hammer strikes, then slides off to the side of the rivet head.

Jig saw circle guide: This is a metal attachment to force the jig saw into a circular cutting path to cut holes in plywood up to two feet in diameter.

Levels: To erect walls, you will need both a carpenter's level and a plumb bob. The plumb bob indicates vertical perpendicular placement.

Measuring Tape: Buy both the 25' metal and the 100' cloth tape. The longer tape is used to lay out markings for erecting the haunted house walls.

Nails: There are three types of nails most often used by prop makers and set builders:

Box nails, which have a thin shank with a large head. They are used for most purposes.

Finishing nails, which are thin and have a very small head that can be hidden easily. They are used where appearance is important.

Duplex nails, or two-headed nails, which have a small space between the two heads and can be easily pulled out. They are used for temporary structures.

Nailset: Pushes the nail below the surface. This makes sanding easier and gives a more finished look.

Perforated Rasp: This tool can be used to trim and shape wood, plastic and hard foam.

Pliers: You should have both slip-joint and locking vise types.

Router: This tool has many uses, primarily for rounding off sharp corners and edges on wood and plastic. It is great for cutting, shaping, etching channels, and creating slots.

Saws: You should get a hacksaw, jig saw, and circular saw. If you can afford it you should consider a band saw, a table saw and a chop saw for cutting studs at various angles. If you cannot afford to buy or rent a chop saw, you will at least need a wood saw and a miter box.

Screwdrivers: Get several standard and a #1 Phillips. Also buy driver bits for your drill. These are 3-inch-long metal rods with screwdriver heads.

You can also buy a magnet that is made to fit onto the bit. This is used to hold a screw onto the bit before plunging it into the material.

Studfinder: Buy the density-sensitive kind rather than the magnetic type. The density studfinder will show the exact location of wood and metal framing studs as well as pipes and conduits.

T-bevel: This device is used to copy and transfer angles.

Three-quarter inch butt chisel: Use for rough notching and trimming of wood and plastic.

Lumber

There are two types of lumber: hardwood (such as maple, cherry and oak) and softwood (such as pine, cedar and spruce). Softwoods, such as pine, are usually used in prop and set construction. They are lightweight and can be worked easily. If you have

a choice, use Idaho or northern white pine. There are other kinds of white pine, but they are heavier due to high water or resin content. Other pines, such as sugar pine, will gum up the cutting tools. Douglas fir and California redwood split more easily. Cedar is brittle and varies in hardness from one piece to another. Spruce, hemlock and most firs will warp badly.

Hardwoods are stronger than softwoods and may be needed for projects where strength is important (such as furniture). Hardwoods also take stain evenly, whereas the large grain of softwood is obvious when stained.

Plywood is laminated sheet wood, usually made from layers of softwoods such as pine or fir. This lamination process increases the strength of the wood. Sometimes plywood is made with an outer layer of hardwood for furniture finishes. A very cheap type of plywood called Plyscord can be used where a good surface is not needed.

Chips and bits of wood are mixed with glue and pressed to form particle board. This is a good cheap material, but it does not tolerate detailed cuts like slots because it chips easily.

Look for lumber that is straight, light and strong. It should have few knots, and what knots there are should be tight (not falling out of the boards).

Lumber comes in stock sizes —1" × 3", 2" × 4", 4" × 4", etc. For a variety of reasons, lumber nowadays nearly always comes smaller than its traditional stated size. For instance, a 2" × 4" is usually 1½" × 3½". Use for rough notching and trimming of wood and plastic.

Be sure in the construction of the sets and corridors that there are no nails, screws or splinters sticking out, and nothing that the customer can trip over.

The Wall Frames

Each frame is made from 2" × 4" studs. (Remember that modern 2" × 4" studs do not measure an actual two inches by four inches.) The final dimensions of this frame are 4' wide by 8' high. It will be about 3" thick with the panel or plywood sheet front. Each frame requires two 96" studs and three 45" studs. You should use wood glue and 3" drywall screws to fasten the studs.

Glue the ends; then drill 2 snug holes for the drywall screws.

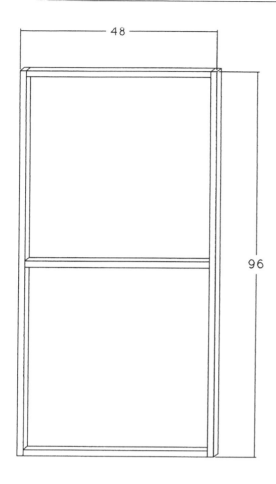

Walls that will need to support objects like paintings or any heavy wall hangings should be made with ¼" sheet plywood.

Some walls, such as background walls, can be made with ⅛" thin sheets of "door skin" or cheap paneling wood. If the ⅛" sheets are used, use a staple gun instead of screws or nails.

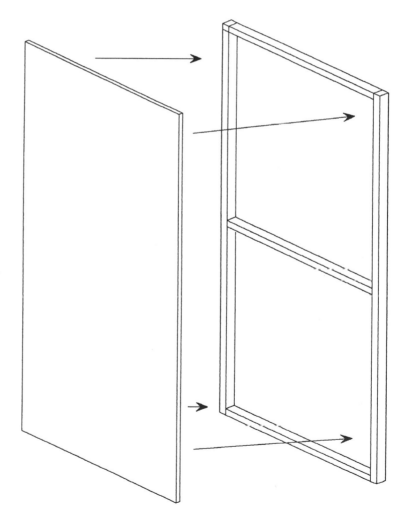

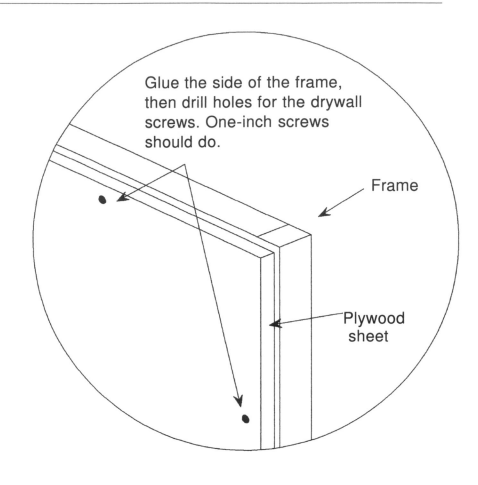

Glue the side of the frame, then drill holes for the drywall screws. One-inch screws should do.

Frame

Plywood sheet

A note on painting: Most of the walls will be painted flat black. Plan on using 0.003 gallons of paint per haunted house square foot. For example, a 2400 square foot haunted house will need about 7.2 gallons of paint for basic wall covering. I recommend spray painting with a rented or borrowed sprayer. If you use a brush or rollers you may need more paint.

Building Temporary Walls

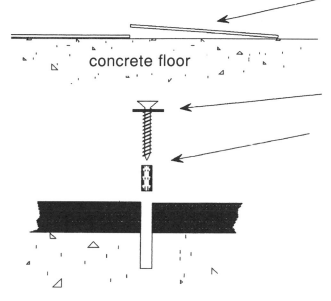

concrete floor

Lay 2" × 4" studs along the floor. These are your base boards. Drill holes in the studs every 3 to 4 feet. These holes should be slightly bigger than the screws.

$\frac{5}{32}$" × $\frac{7}{8}$" fender washer

Use 3" drywall screws with a plastic or metal "anchor" to fix the stud to the floor. These anchors can be bought from a hardware store. Use a hammer drill to drill holes in concrete.

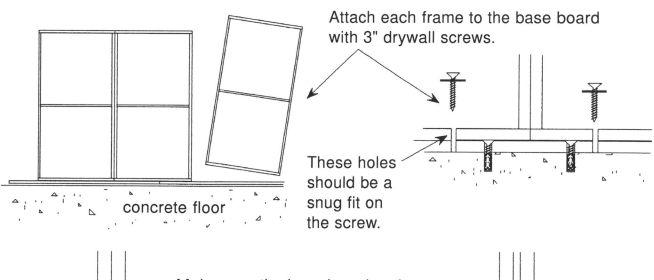

Attach each frame to the base board with 3" drywall screws.

These holes should be a snug fit on the screw.

concrete floor

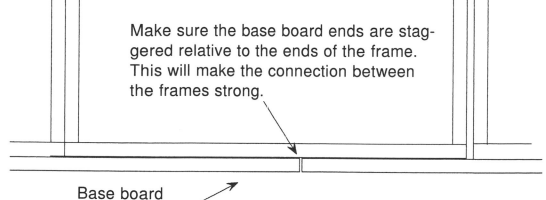

Make sure the base board ends are staggered relative to the ends of the frame. This will make the connection between the frames strong.

Base board

Again using 3" drywall
screws, attach top
boards across the top
of the frames.

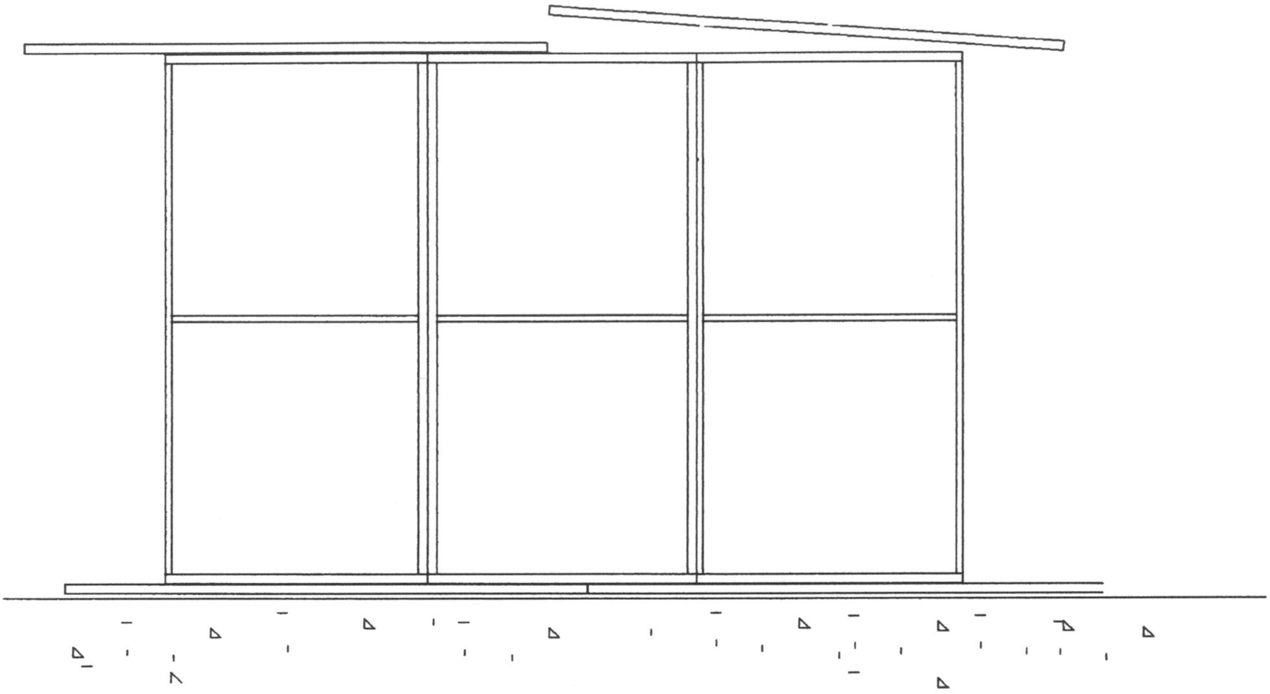

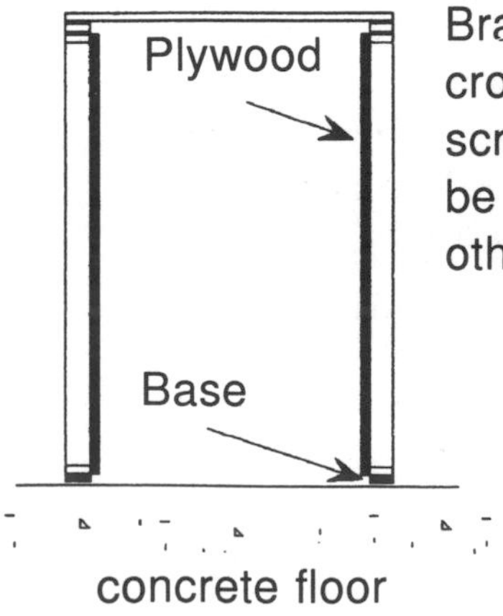

Make sure the top board ends are staggered
relative to the ends of the frame. This will make
the connection between the frames strong.

Plywood

Base

concrete floor

Brace the top of the walls with a
cross board with 3" drywall
screws. These top braces must
be at least 8 feet apart from each
other.

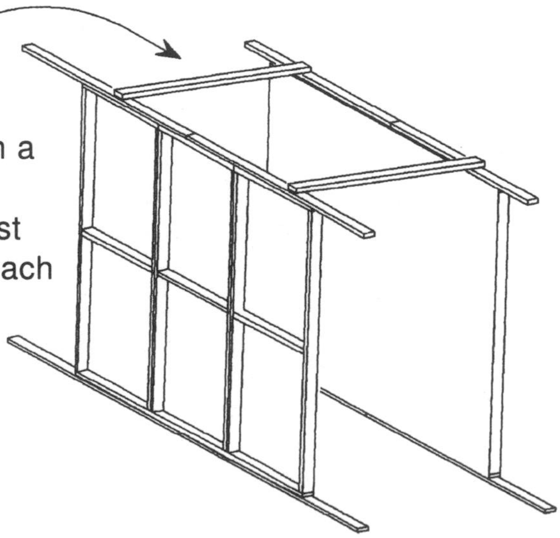

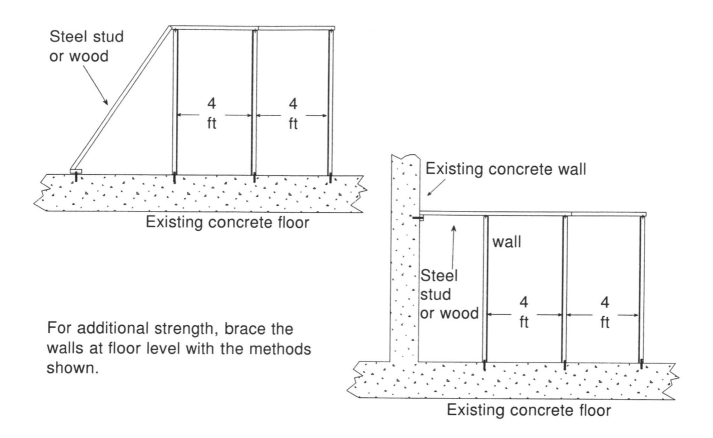

Steel stud or wood

4 ft   4 ft

Existing concrete floor

For additional strength, brace the walls at floor level with the methods shown.

Existing concrete wall

wall

Steel stud or wood

4 ft   4 ft

Existing concrete floor

Electrical Cord Organization

When laying out electrical cables and wires, never let them just lie on the ground. Try to run them across the tops of the walls you will be building.

Professionals run such cables in "cable trays." These are like water gutters that hang from the ceiling, attach to the walls or sit on top of the walls. You can make your own cable trays with the metal studs that are normally used for framing walls. These metal studs are eight feet long, shaped like a water gutter with holes, and cost only about a dollar apiece.

If nothing else, at least use tie wraps to bundle wires into larger cables. Then run the cables across walls by resting them on screws, nails or hooks. You must make every effort to organize the wires and cables so that they are not just a bird's nest of cords, and make sure the customers cannot touch any wires no matter how you arrange them. The fire marshals will be impressed and more likely to pass you in your inspection.

Do not use "octopus plugs," or splitters, with your extension cords; use only power strips with internal fuses. Shop around for these because the price will range from $5 to $30 apiece. The cheaper ones are fine, as long as they have internal reset fuses.

WRONG   RIGHT

Gather up loose wires and electrical cords into one cable and bind them together with "tiewraps."

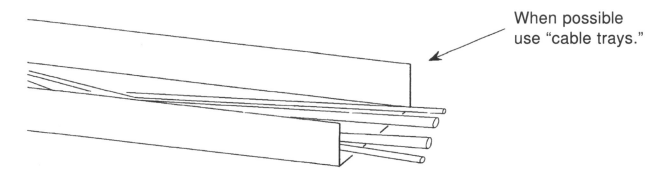

When possible use "cable trays."

Screw the trays to the top of the walls.

Run cables on pegs made from screws or nails.

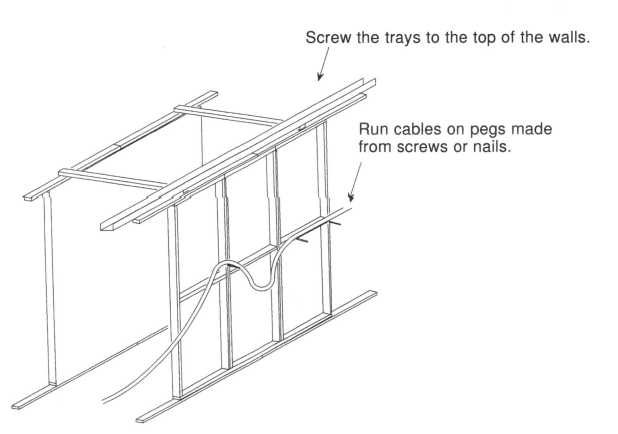

3. Basic Effects

Please, please, *please* keep away from clichéd effects and bad "boo technology." Peeled-grape eyeballs, spaghetti brains, alien spaceships, mad scientist labs, and horror movie characters jumping out of dark corners and screaming in the customer's face are the result of uncreative, lazy development. Remember, you want to be better than the other haunted houses. You can charge any amount of money as long as the customer feels your presentation is worth it. One good test is to imagine how you would feel if you paid to see a movie that used your effect. Would you be getting your money's worth? Think "theme" and "story continuity." Ask yourself questions like, "Why would a robot be running around in a house that was possessed by spirits?" "Would the Creature from the Black Lagoon really hang out in the bathtub of a haunted house?" If you saw these concepts in a horror movie, you would giggle, not shiver.

You will have to decide if the house you build will be "soft" or "hardcore." Hardcore houses are more bloody and horrific, while soft houses are spooky and entertain with illusions. The hardcore houses draw more teenage customers but tend to be locked into a particular market. If you design eerie effects that the whole family can enjoy, the parents pay for three to five tickets instead of just two. Plus, good soft houses draw less fire from community watchdogs.

Magicians have classified their illusions into 19 basic categories. This is useful for organizing and inventing effects. Illusions for a haunted house can be divided into seven basic categories: appearance or vanish, transformation, penetration, animation or levitation, physical paradox, sensory assault, and threatening object. Some effects will fall into more than one category.

Appearance or Vanish

An *appearance* is the formation of an object or creature from empty space, such as a spirit coming into existence before your eyes, or a ghost's face appearing in a mirror. The opposite effect is a *vanish*.

Basic Methods

1. Object or creature taken from or taken to secret hiding place while attention is diverted elsewhere.

2. Object or creature brought from or taken to secret hiding place, very quickly.

3. Image appears or disappears by means of reflection using light control.

4. Object or creature revealed or hidden with cover that blends into the background; or object or creature blends into the background; background is then changed.

5. Object produced or destroyed by chemical means.

6. Object or creature produced or removed by optical projection.

7. Object or creature is disguised (to vanish), or disguise is removed (to appear).

8. Expandable object taken from or collapsed into secret hiding place.

9. Object catapulted or thrown into or out of place of appearance or disappearance.

Example

The Mirror Ghost (see page 34)

Transformation

An object or creature changes state or form; for example, a pretty young woman changes into an old demonic hag, or a man melts into a skeleton.

Basic Methods

Although the effect seems to be different from appearance or vanish, many transformations can be achieved by making one subject appear and another vanish, using the methods previously described.

1. Chemical change.

2. Optical projection.

3. Disguise is put on or taken off.

4. Change in relative surroundings.

5. Dual identity (an object which may assume two identities, such as the optical illusion that shows an old woman and a young woman in the same drawing).

Examples

Girl Change (see page 35); The Rotting Corpse (see pages 36–37)

Penetration

An object or creature passes through a solid object; for example, a hand reaches through a painting or brick wall.

Basic Methods

1. Duplicate penetrator used; as one vanishes, the other one appears on either side of the obstacle.

2. One penetrator used with a secret passageway.

3. Penetrator is an optical projection.

4. Obstacle is an optical projection.

5. Penetrator is collapsible.

Examples

The Grabber (see page 38); The Parasite (see pages 39–40)

Animation or Levitation

A nonliving object moves or is suspended in the air by some unseen force — a doll moves as if alive, furniture floats in the air, a door opens by itself.

Basic Methods

1. Invisible connection to source of power (thread or wire).

2. Concealed connection to source of power through stand, support, or accessory.

    A. Support concealed at the back or side of object.

    B. Support concealed through reflection.

    C. Support concealed by camouflage (such as black support against a black background).

3. Built-in source of power (clockwork, electric motor, rubber band, etc.).

4. Chemical source of power.

5. Gravity.

6. Optical illusion by variation of light and shade.

7. Magnetic attraction.

8. Atmospheric pressure.

    A. Secret blast of air or suction.

    B. Lighter-than-air object disguised as heavy object.

Examples

The Demonic Doll (see page 41); The Seance Room (see pages 42–43)

Physical Paradox

An object or creature in a state or form that defies normal physics, like a bottomless pit, an unseasonable storm, a fire without heat, a headless man walking around still alive, or a creature that does not have a reflection in a mirror.

Basic Methods

Technically, all the illusions described so far could be put under this category; anything that seems to contradict physical laws is a physical paradox. There is, however, a definite group of illusions that particularly seem to defy normal physical conditions. Many makeup techniques and special effect costumes will create cardinal effects. Other effects are made possible through the use of mirrors, optical devices, and methods described under other categories.

Examples

The Bottomless Pit (see page 44); Fire Illusion (see page 45); The Headless Butler (see pages 46–47); The Holographic Ghost (see pages 48–49); Pepper's Ghost (see pages 50–51); The Undead (see page 52); The Ghost in the Machine (see pages 53–54); The Will-o'-the-Wisp (see page 55)

Sensory Assault

I call this "boo technology": a sudden or loud sound, a cold shot of air, a flash of light, a bad smell, or a gory, unpleasant, or shocking sight. This category is easy to overuse. Unpleasant sights would include a beating heart and moving dismembered hand on a dinner table, or weird paintings of macabre scenes or creatures.

Basic Methods

Anything that startles one or more of the customer's five senses will get a reflex action, but proper care should be taken to make the "boo technology" *relevant* to the haunted house. By *relevant* I mean consistent with the customers' impression that they are in a haunted Victorian house, castle, graveyard or whatever "theme" you have chosen. The idea is to not break the customers' suspension of disbelief.

Here's an example of an irrelevant "boo": Your customer is making her way through a moonlit graveyard. The "tales from the crypt" theme song is playing loud enough to feel — but not too loud to hear the baying wolves in the distance. The smell of fresh earth permeates the air. She catches some movement from the corner of her eye, when suddenly a maniac clown from outer space rushes at her with a snake violently snapping to and fro like a fleshy bullwhip! The demonic clown laughs, says "gotcha" and walks back to its hiding place. (I actually saw this happen once!)

Sure, the customer might scream from being startled. But a loud buzzer would have done the same thing. And now she is reminded that she is in a theater set with human beings dressed in costumes, because the maniac's appearance is out of place. It does not carry the theme. (Why would the clown be trying to attack the customer? To feed his pet snake?) A better scenario would have been to have a zombie burst through

the ground and try and attack her, but because the undead creature is still half buried in the ground, he can't quite reach her. The zombie cries out, "Brains, I must eat your brains."

Examples

The Bug Box (see page 56); The Drop "Boo" (see page 57); The Living Heart (see pages 58–59); The Pop-up "Boo" (see page 60); The Monster in the Painting (see page 61)

Threatening Object

An object or creature that presents a perceived threat or danger, like a rattlesnake, a spider, a bat, or a possessed maniac with a chainsaw. This is another overused category.

Basic Methods

To invoke the fear reflex from your customers, rely on standard phobias. Subjects that appear to be dangerous are rubber or stuffed animals and insects. If rubber subjects are used, take care to obtain high quality items; cheap rubber snakes, for instance, do not allow the suspension of disbelief you need. I like to use taxidermy animals because they possess the most realism. Sometimes a good artist can repaint some of the cheap items to appear more realistic. Another trick to make rubber props look like living flesh is to make them glisten with a mist spray of silicon liquid or water. You can also use darkness and distance to help make an object look more realistic. Rubber knives and spiders can be effective if you spend the money for realistic items or paint the item to look better. Chrome spray paint can make a plastic toy knife look very real. The chapter on prop making will describe the best methods of painting rubber.

Examples

The Hovering Bat (see pages 62–63); The Scurrying Rat (see pages 64–65); The Snake in the Wall (see page 66); The Dropping Spiders (see page 67)

Appearance: The Mirror Ghost

Walking to a bend in the hallway, the customer is startled by the glowing image of a spirit face that suddenly appears in a fancy mirror.

To accomplish this trick you will need to make a two-way mirror. First, find a large, fancy picture frame. Have a piece of glass cut to fit. Take the glass to an auto tinter and have it silver-tinted. It may need to have two layers put on. This tinting will make the glass into a two-way mirror.

The two-way mirror is mounted over a hole in the wall. Standing behind the wall against black curtains is the operator with water-based fluorescent paint on her face, neck and hair. A black light is mounted *below* the hole, facing up, and covered with a wood flap. By lifting this flap, the operator appears in the mirror as a "spirit." Be sure that the wood flap does not get hot enough to burn!

Black light is covered with a wood flap. It is lifted by the operator to reveal the "spirit." This is better than turning the black light on and off.

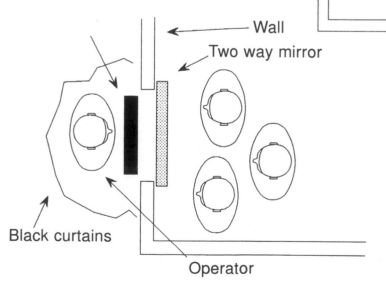

Transformation: Girl Change (Girl Transforms into Hag)

The customers come into a room. A pretty young girl in an old-fashioned dress is standing there. She blocks the exit until everyone is in the room. She suddenly says, "There is something strange about this house!" Then, right before their eyes, she screams and turns into a hideous old woman as if possessed by a spirit. Just as mysteriously, she suddenly turns back into the pretty young girl and turns to open the exit for the customers to continue.

This effect is done with red makeup, a red light, and a blue light. The exact shade of the lights and the makeup may take a little experimenting to get them right. The red makeup is used instead of black to create lines and shading on the girl's face. When the red light is on, the red makeup will not be visible. But when the blue light is switched on, the red makeup will appear dark brown or black, making the old-age effects visible. You should use colored flood lights connected to a single-throw double pole switch. This switch can be obtained at a hardware store. It will allow you to turn off the red light and at the same time turn on the blue light with the flick of just one switch. The dress should be white, and *no red or blue props or background should be used.*

Dramatic eyebrows

Red paint streaking a long white wig.

"Crowsfeet" and age lines around the eyes.

Enlarge the nostrils by darkening the edges.

Use red tooth wax to "black out" some of the teeth. Put red food coloring onto the tongue.

Age spots

Make up all exposed flesh.

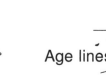

Age lines

Red nail polish.

Transformation:
The Rotting Corpse

Man in a coffin.

Skeleton in a coffin.

The customers watch as a man in a coffin melts into a bony skeleton.

This is done with a plate of glass and two lights on dimmer switches. The man can be living or just a mannequin.

(continued on next page)

(The Rotting Corpse, continued)

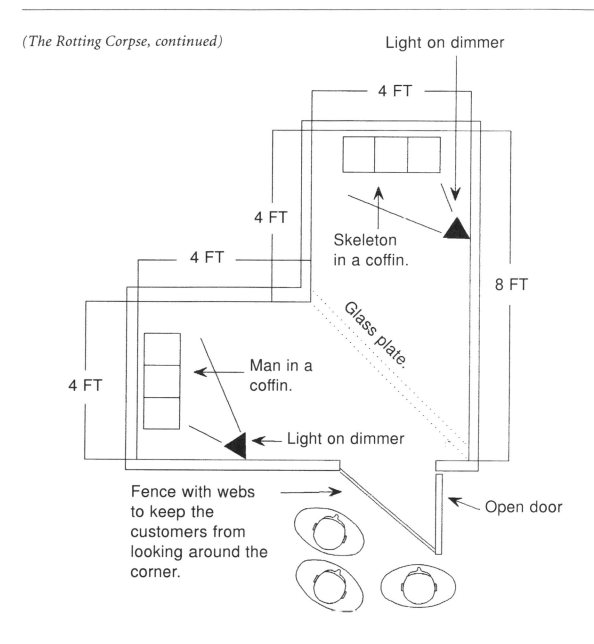

The man and skeleton are placed on opposite sides of a clear glass plate such as an old sliding glass door. Begin by illuminating the side that is outside the customers' field of vision (the "man" side). The image will reflect onto the glass. Now, darken that side while bringing up the lights on the other, which will show *through* the glass. The operator must turn down one dimmer and turn up the other at the same time. Be sure the placement of the two subjects is identical on either side of the glass. This setup is known as a "blue room."

Penetration: The Grabber

An abstract painting hangs in a hallway with other works of art. But as the customer passes, a hand suddenly reaches out from this painting as if to grab a victim. (Never grab customers. It's dangerous.) Just as quickly it disappears back into the painting.

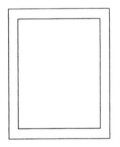

First buy an old picture frame from a thrift store. Be sure it is wood and very strong.

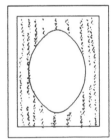

Cut a plywood insert that has a decorator round or elliptical hole. Paint it to match the wood frame, or spray-paint the entire insert and frame with gold or copper paint.

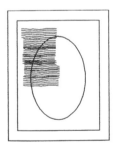  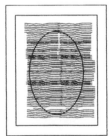

Buy two cheap brooms with plastic bristles. Try to get the bristles as long as you can afford. Cut them and glue them in layers to create a two-part curtain on the back of the frame.

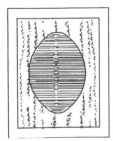

Flip the frame over and paint a multicolored picture in an abstract style. Attach this over a hole in the wall with drywall screws.

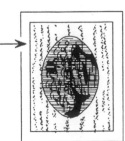

Penetration: The Parasite

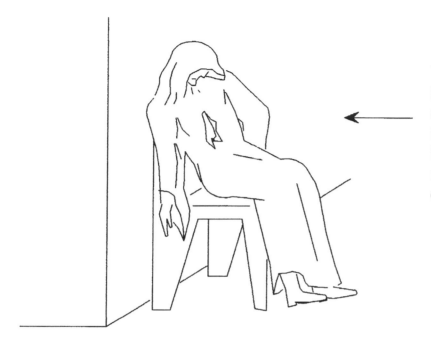

The customers have to walk by this scary-looking man in a robe. He looks hurt, with a large wound in his chest. His head is down, but it slowly rises to stare at the closest customer.

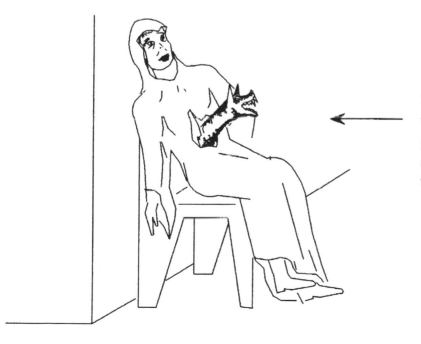

Suddenly something jumps from his chest. A horrible parasite with fangs snaps at the customers as they walk by.

(continued on next page)

(The Parasite, continued)

This effect is done with a headless dummy and a hand puppet. The dummy is set in a chair against the wall. The operator sticks his head through the wall into the dummy's hood. The puppet must be as realistic as possible. You can buy these puppets at most novelty stores.

It is a good idea to attach the dummy to the wall to help keep it from slipping.

Animation: The Demonic Doll

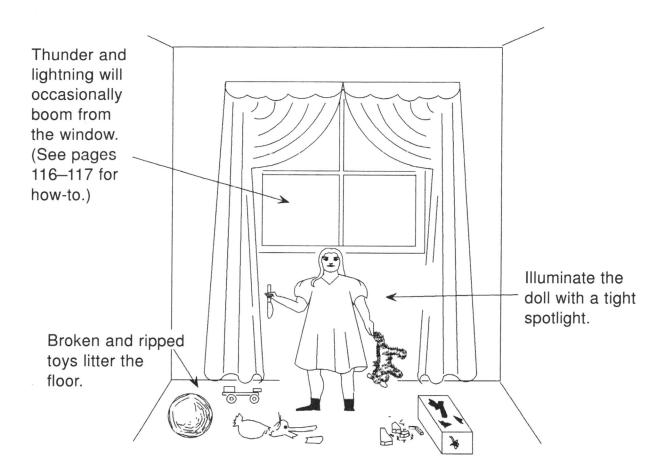

Thunder and lightning will occasionally boom from the window. (See pages 116–117 for how-to.)

Illuminate the doll with a tight spotlight.

Broken and ripped toys litter the floor.

The customers pass by a playroom where a little doll has come to life! It has a knife in its hand and has destroyed the other toys. The doll's eyes and mouth move while it giggles and says things like, "Let's play hospital," or, "I want to play autopsy."

This is a very effective set on its own, but you could add a "dead" or "hurt" little boy just lying on the floor. The doll is a toy called "Cricket." I bought mine from a thrift store, but you may have to buy it new. It has built-in automatronics. A normal cassette tape with a little girl's voice activates the eye and mouth movements. You will need to record your own doll voice on an endless loop tape. Make sure you record on both tracks. The left speaker track operates the doll movements. The right track plays through the doll's one speaker in the torso.

The doll requires batteries and will eat them up fast, so keep extras on hand. The company that makes these dolls is Playmate Toys, 16200 South Trojan Way, La Mirada CA 90638, phone number (714) 739-1929.

Levitation: The Seance Room

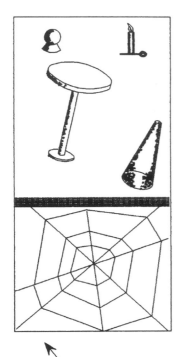

Customers can peer into this room and see objects floating in the air as if a seance has called spirits to move them. Eerie music plays in the room.

Fence painted black, then camouflaged with spiderwebs.

Operators are dressed all in black with hoods and gloves. They use black poles to control the "floating" objects.

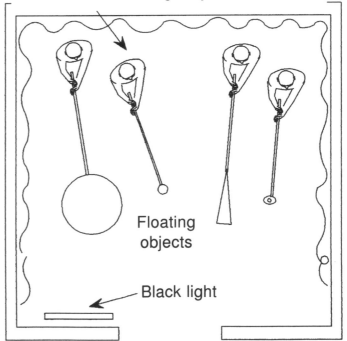

Floating objects

Black light

This 15' deep room is lined with flat black curtains or the walls are painted black. The floor where the operators stand must be painted black.

(continued on next page)

(The Seance Room, continued)

All the floating objects are made of light cardboard, foam, or other light materials, then painted with white paint. When dry, they are painted again, this time with fluorescent yellow paint. Each object is then attached to a black 8' pole.

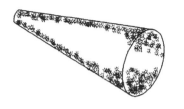

This spirit horn is simply rolled construction paper. If PVC pipe is attached to one end, the operator can speak through it into the horn.

This table is made from hard foam that can be bought in the proper shapes from a craft store.

This candle is made of hard foam with a "flame" made from a cotton puff that is stretched and painted with streaks of fluorescent paint.

This crystal ball is made from a balloon, with a paper cup glued to the bottom.

Physical Paradox: The Bottomless Pit

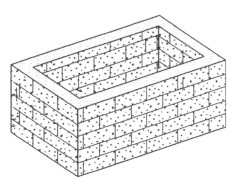

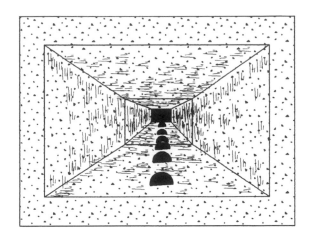

Customers pass by this bottomless pit and peer into its depths. They can hear someone yelling for help as the trapped victim's voice echoes up from the well.

This is accomplished with an old principle of mirror reflection. You will need to make a two-way mirror from a plate of glass that has been silver-tinted. You can take the plate to an auto window tinter and ask them to do it for $10.

Reflector:
Plywood with flashing

2½ inch

Attach flashing to the wood with a staple gun.

Paint rocks or bricks inside and outside of the wood frame box. The box can be constructed from 1" × 2" pine studs covered with door skins.

Tinted glass with the reflective side down.

Mirror with the reflective side up.

Reflector is set against the glass.

Low-watt light bulb with reflector fixed above.

Sound effects speaker placed in cavity of the box.

Physical Paradox: Fire Illusion

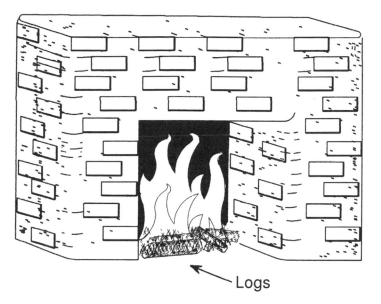

Logs

A fake fireplace can be improved with a fake fire. It is done with a large white sheet of lightweight fabric, like silk. An oscillation fan and two amber lights behind the fake fireplace will create the illusion.

Lightweight white sheet stapled to the back of the fake fireplace. The sheet should have a little "play."

Staples

You should place patches of duct tape over the staples to prevent them from ripping the fabric.

Wall has opening for fireplace.

From the back, spray-paint the edges with flat black paint. Do not let it run. Do It in several light coats.

Experiment with different angles for the fan.

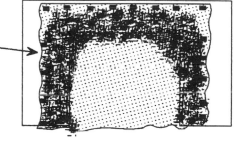

Fake fireplace

White sheet

The two lights should be two different shades of yellow or amber.

Physical Paradox: The Headless Butler

Walls are painted white.

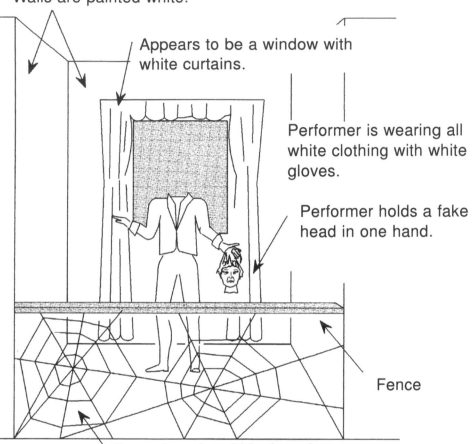

Appears to be a window with white curtains.

Performer is wearing all white clothing with white gloves.

Performer holds a fake head in one hand.

Fence

Fence is painted black and camouflaged with spiderwebs.

Performer is wearing a black hood that cannot be seen against the black background with the proper lighting.

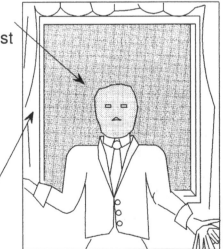

The window is actually black velour or felt. Then it is trimmed with white wood to simulate a window frame.

(continued on next page)

(The Headless Butler, continued)

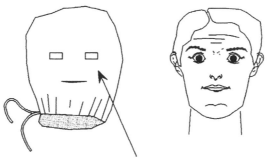

The hood has a slit for the nose and two small holes for the eyes. A drawstring is sewn at the base to pull the base of the hood snug against the neck.

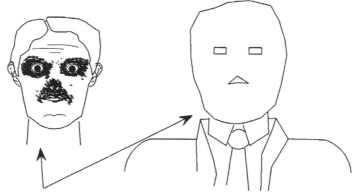

Cover the nose and eyes with black makeup. Tuck the base of the hood into the collar of the white shirt. When the performer turns toward the customers he should close his eyes.

The light is directed toward the customers so that the performer is illuminated just enough to be clearly visible, but the black hood is invisible. The light should be on a dimmer and on a switch. The dimmer will help to adjust the brightness, and the switch turns the light off to make the customers move on. *The performer cannot move toward the customers.*

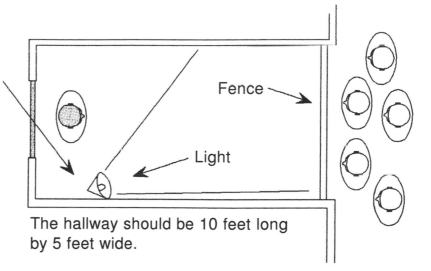

The hallway should be 10 feet long by 5 feet wide.

Physical Paradox: The Holographic Ghost

As the customers approach the haunted house, a giant 3D image of a spirit head floats in the air over the front yard or on the roof. I invented this amazing illusion in 1987 for the city of Laverne's haunted house in California. It was great for drawing in new customers. It is an image from a 500-watt slide projector on the *back* of a wall of water. The water wall is made by a special nozzle. This illusion can only be done at night.

Hand-paint a face on a glass slide by painting in the non-image areas with black acrylic paint. You cannot use a normal slide as the dark regions will not completely black out the projector light.

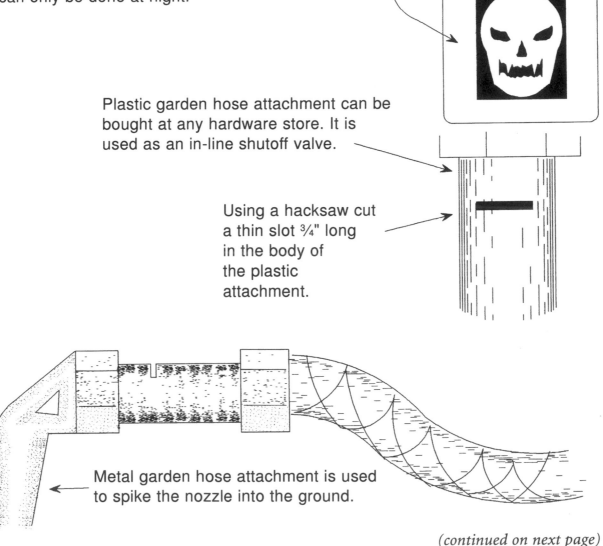

Plastic garden hose attachment can be bought at any hardware store. It is used as an in-line shutoff valve.

Using a hacksaw cut a thin slot ¾" long in the body of the plastic attachment.

Metal garden hose attachment is used to spike the nozzle into the ground.

(continued on next page)

(The Holographic Ghost, continued)

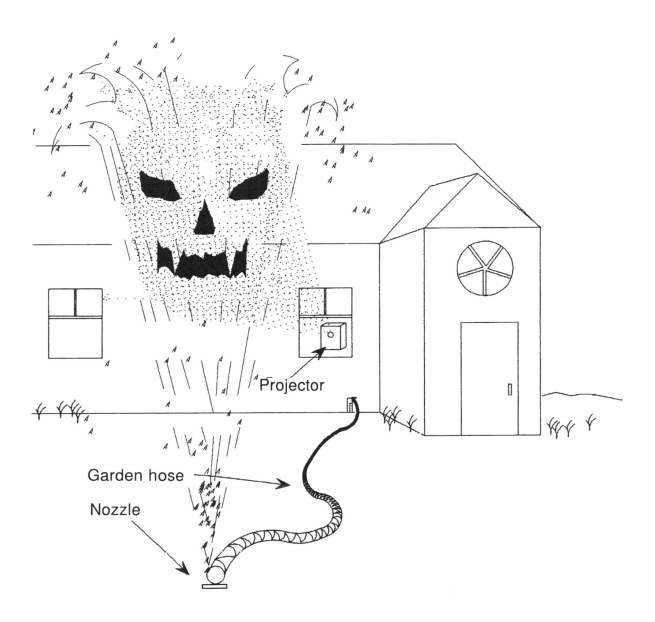

Projector

Garden hose

Nozzle

The projector is placed in a window, pointing out toward the spot where the water will spray. Turn on the projector, then turn on the water.

Physical Paradox: Pepper's Ghost

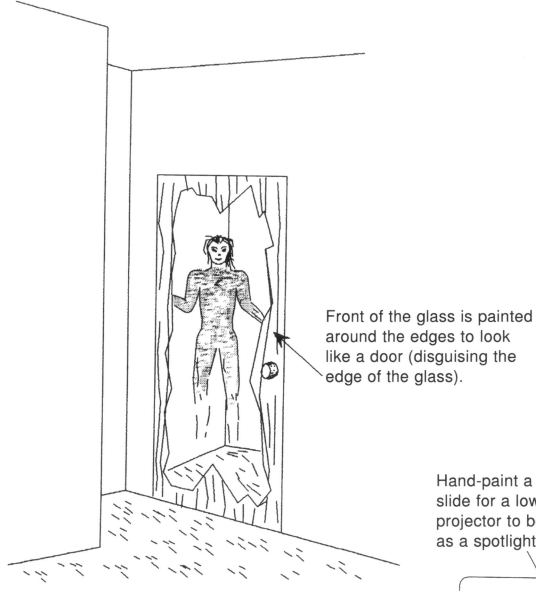

Front of the glass is painted around the edges to look like a door (disguising the edge of the glass).

Hand-paint a glass slide for a low-watt projector to be used as a spotlight.

The customers see a 3D image of the upper torso and head of a ghost. It is floating behind a door with a large hole. This illusion is based on the "Pepper's Ghost" principle. It dates back over 100 years. It is done with a glass door or a sheet of ¼" clear plastic, painted around the edges to look like wood. A fake door handle is glued to the front.

(continued on next page)

(Pepper's Ghost, continued)

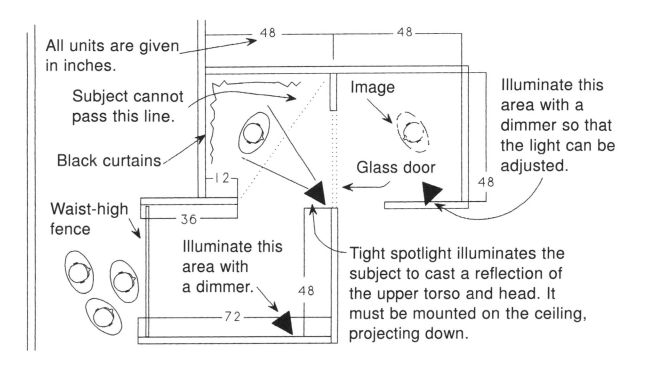

The lighting is critical for this effect. There are three light sources: the spot, and two lights on *separate* dimmers. You will need to adjust the lights for the maximum effect.

Physical Paradox: The Undead

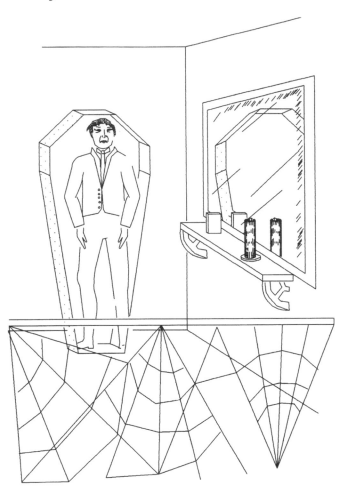

The customers can see a reflection of the room in the mirror, but the vampire has no reflection. The mirror is really a bug screen stapled to a hole in the wall. It is framed to look like a mirror. Behind the wall, visible through the hole, is a duplicate room. Make sure the light in both rooms matches, and check that the furnishings are set in "mirrored" positions. The vampire can be just a dressed-up dummy. Make it look like it is asleep. The fence will keep the customers from looking directly into the "mirror."

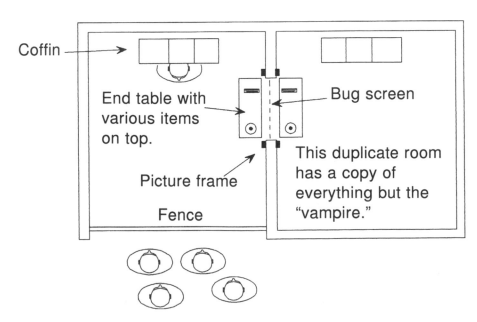

Coffin

End table with various items on top.

Bug screen

Picture frame

This duplicate room has a copy of everything but the "vampire."

Fence

Physical Paradox: The Ghost in the Machine

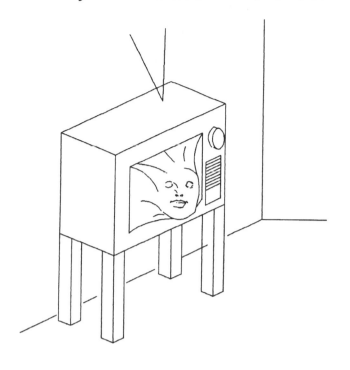

As the customers walk by this eerie television, a face stretches the TV screen and protrudes forward.

Wipe a glass plate with KY jelly, then brush several layers of untinted latex across the plate.

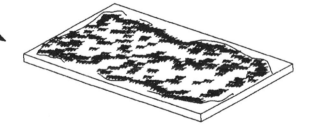

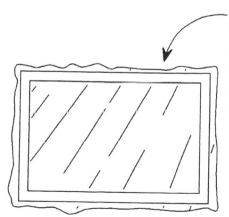

When the latex rubber sheet has dried, remove it from the glass and wash the KY off. Then stretch it across a wooden frame that has been covered with contact cement. With a staple gun, secure the edges. Cover the staples with more latex to help keep them from splitting the rubber.

(continued on next page)

(The Ghost in the Machine, continued)

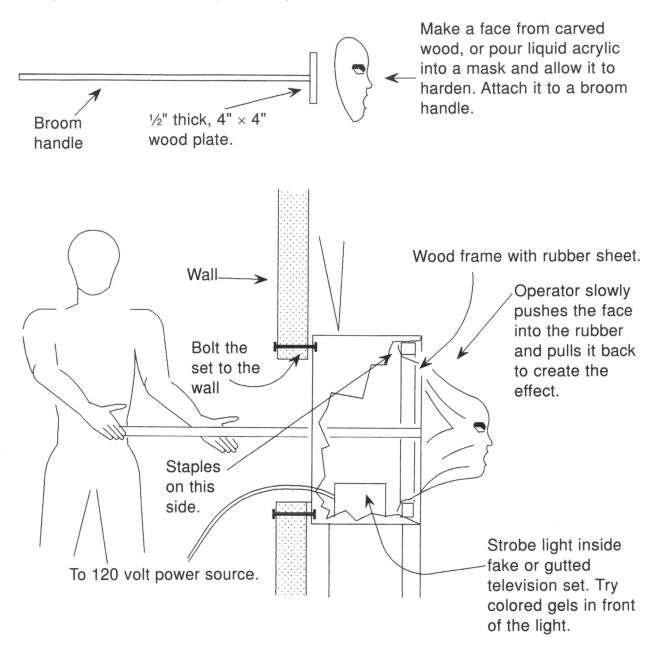

Make a face from carved wood, or pour liquid acrylic into a mask and allow it to harden. Attach it to a broom handle.

Broom handle

½" thick, 4" × 4" wood plate.

Wall

Bolt the set to the wall

Staples on this side.

To 120 volt power source.

Wood frame with rubber sheet.

Operator slowly pushes the face into the rubber and pulls it back to create the effect.

Strobe light inside fake or gutted television set. Try colored gels in front of the light.

Physical Paradox: The Will-o'-the-Wisp

Fence

The customers can peer into the room to see a will-o'-the-wisp floating around the room. It twinkles and dances in the air like dozens of fireflies.

Like most good tricks, this eerie effect is accomplished with simple props and a lot of showmanship.

You will need to buy a small, lightweight, low-power (20 watts or so) slide projector. The kind sold at toy stores for children work great! Make a slide out of flashing or a tin pie plate. Punch tiny holes in a small round group. Then hang white yarn in long strips from the ceiling of the room to the furniture tops and floor. The result is a scattered wall about 2 feet wide that spans from one side of the room to the opposite corner in a half-circle pattern.

Thin tin slide with little holes clustered in a round group.

Do not pass this line.

The operator swings the projector in medium-speed sweeps and figure eights.

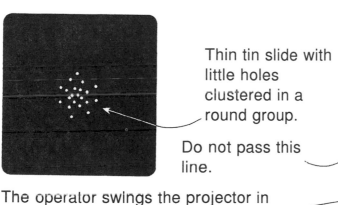

White walls

Light beams

White yarn hanging from the ceiling

The room must be as dark as possible, with just enough light from the doorway to illuminate the furniture and white walls in the room.

Sensory Assault: The Bug Box

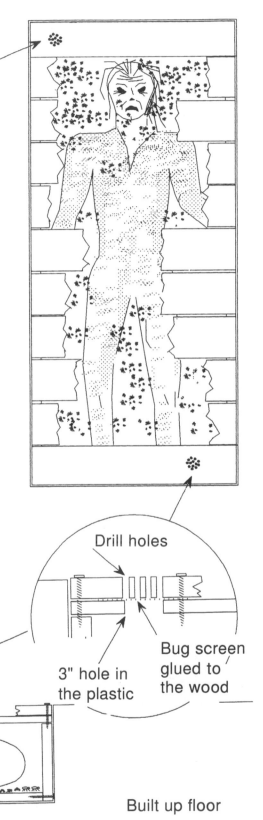

Drillhole

The customers have to step over this horror. Beneath the broken floor boards is a decomposing body with hundreds of bugs crawling all over it.

If the haunted house floor is not hollow, you will have to build up a false floor, in which case the customers will see this effect after climbing a short ramp. Make sure the box is bug-tight. The air holes will use bug screen to keep them in. The corpse is a dummy of course, and most of the bugs are realistic plastic bugs from a novelty shop or a bait shop. But the illusion is completed with the use of real crickets that are obtained from a pet store. These crickets cost from 5 to 10 cents apiece. Twenty dollars' worth is enough to make the fake bugs look real as the real bugs crawl around. You may want to put a small dish of water in the box for the bugs. The clear plastic top could be hinged to make dumping the bugs easier. Or you can just funnel them in through the 3" air hole in the plastic, then screw down the wood with the bug screen. The bugs should last a week, so put them in last.

Drill holes

3" hole in the plastic

Bug screen glued to the wood

This "unbreakable" clear plastic can be bought at hardware stores. It is used to replace broken windows.

Built up floor

Sensory Assault: The Drop "Boo"

A large hole in the wall exposes the wood frame and chicken wire. When the customer takes a closer look a ghoul drops down, slamming into the chicken wire. This one will make them jump out of their skins! It combines a sudden movement with an instinctive fear of onrushing attack.

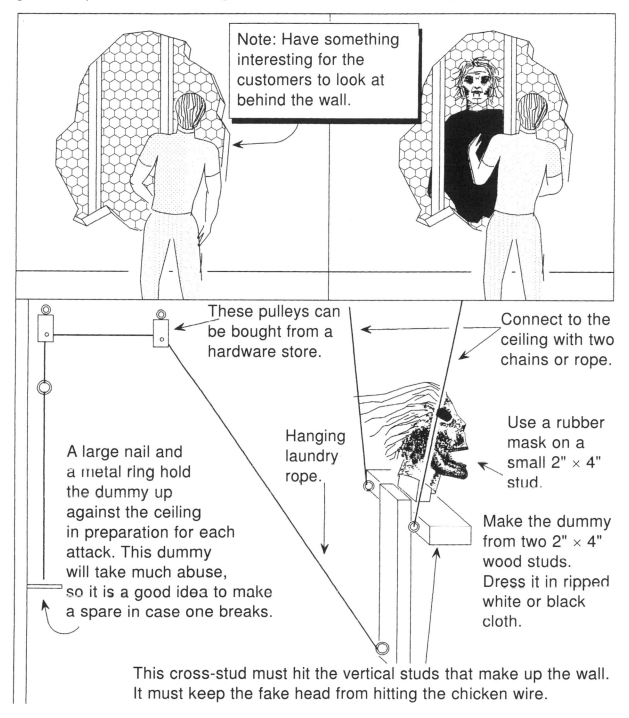

Note: Have something interesting for the customers to look at behind the wall.

These pulleys can be bought from a hardware store.

Connect to the ceiling with two chains or rope.

A large nail and a metal ring hold the dummy up against the ceiling in preparation for each attack. This dummy will take much abuse, so it is a good idea to make a spare in case one breaks.

Hanging laundry rope.

Use a rubber mask on a small 2" × 4" stud.

Make the dummy from two 2" × 4" wood studs. Dress it in ripped white or black cloth.

This cross-stud must hit the vertical studs that make up the wall. It must keep the fake head from hitting the chicken wire.

Sensory Assault: The Living Heart

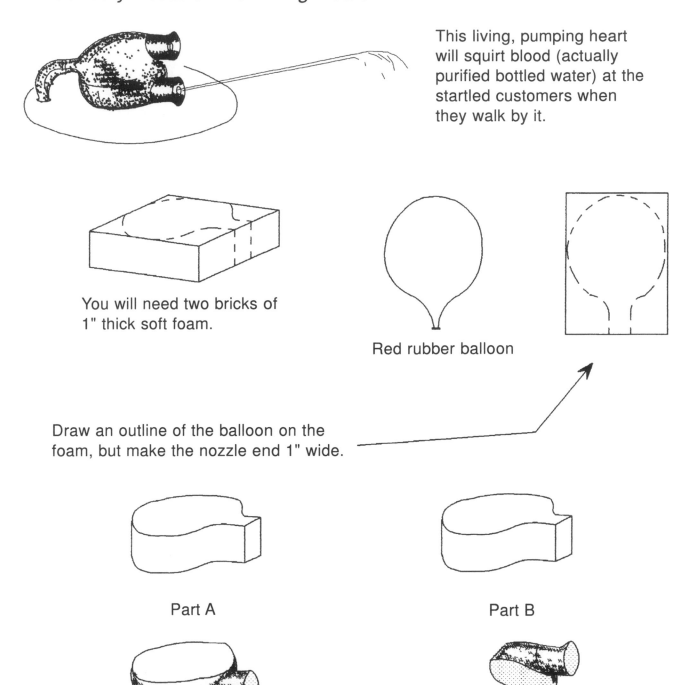

This living, pumping heart will squirt blood (actually purified bottled water) at the startled customers when they walk by it.

You will need two bricks of 1" thick soft foam.

Red rubber balloon

Draw an outline of the balloon on the foam, but make the nozzle end 1" wide.

Part A

Part B

Carve the foam parts into "drumstick" shapes with a flat side. The ball end of part B will be smaller than A.

(continued on next page)

(The Living Heart, continued)

Glue and tape (using electrical tape) a 6' long, ¼" wide vinyl tube to the balloon. This tube will provide air to the balloon to make the heart "pump." To provide the heart with water to squirt, plug a separate 6' tube at one end with hot glue and puncture the plug with a hot needle to create a restricted nozzle. Drill a hole through part A of the foam heart and insert the punctured tube through the back end of the heart to the nozzle end (the artery). Assemble the heart using a little contact cement. The balloon goes between parts A and B and is partially exposed. Now, coat the entire heart with red-tinted latex rubber. Bind the two tubes together with electrical tape. The red latex skin should cover the tubes from the heart down 8 inches.

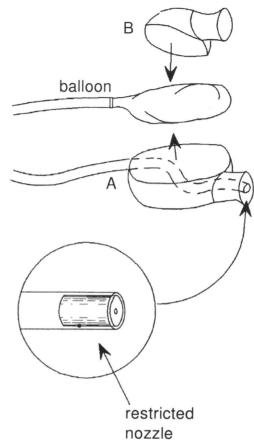

B

balloon

A

restricted
nozzle

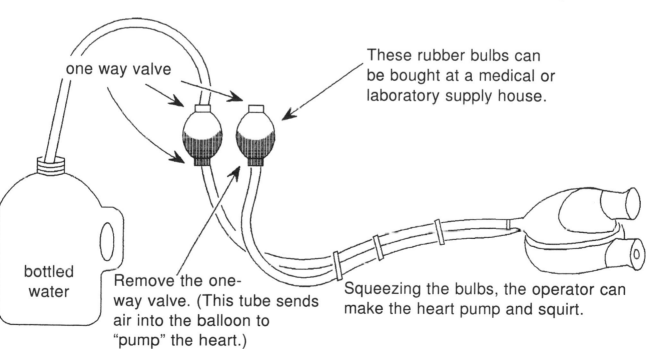

one way valve

These rubber bulbs can
be bought at a medical or
laboratory supply house.

bottled
water

Remove the one-
way valve. (This tube sends
air into the balloon to
"pump" the heart.)

Squeezing the bulbs, the operator can
make the heart pump and squirt.

Sensory Assault: The Pop-up "Boo"

The customers' curiosity compels them to get a closer look at the "dead guy" in the coffin. They may expect it to be an actor in a mask ready to sit up and yell. But they won't expect what happens next. Suddenly from the chest of the corpse a ghoul covered in blood, with intestines hanging from its shoulders, springs up, clutching for its next victim! (Remember: Never actually grab a customer.)

Construct a coffin from light wood. (See "Base Frames" under "Some Basic Props," page 91.) It sits on a cloth-draped table. Both the coffin and the table have holes cut in them to allow passage for the actor.

Construct a simple wood box with hinged flaps to fit inside the coffin. Paint the box completely black and mount a fake head on one end. The box is bottomless but should be attached to the table and the coffin with angle brackets.

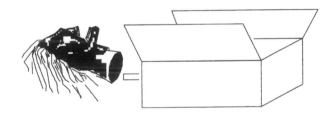

Cut an old dress coat in half and glue each side to the box and flaps. You may want to use padding to round out this fake body. Stuff a pair of dress pants and attach to the box.

Sensory Assault: The Monster in the Painting

As the customers walk through this hallway of hanging portraits, one of the paintings catches their attention. When they stop to take a closer look, the painting suddenly opens to reveal a monster! This is a simple but startling "boo" effect.

All you will need is a picture frame and an interesting painting. A gothic-looking painting of a half-clothed woman will normally stop the males in the group. Mount the frame on a hole cut in the wall. Then mount the portrait to a plywood "door." Attach this door with hinges so the portrait looks normal in the frame. You may want to use a locking latch to hold the door to keep it closed when not in use.

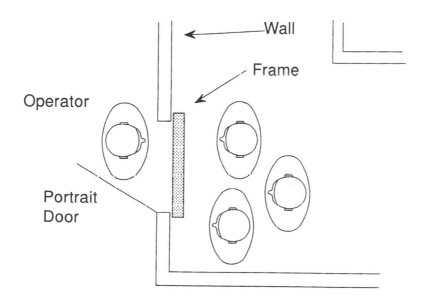

Threatening Object: The Hovering Bat

A bat with fluttering wings appears to hover over the passing customer's head.

This flying bird toy can be bought at novelty or toy stores.

Cut the wings to look bat-shaped. Use plumber's putty to reshape the head into a more batlike face. Use toothpicks for fangs and red sequins for the eyes. Cover with a thin flex-glue skin and paint black. The wings may need pilot ink.

(continued on next page)

(The Hovering Bat, continued)

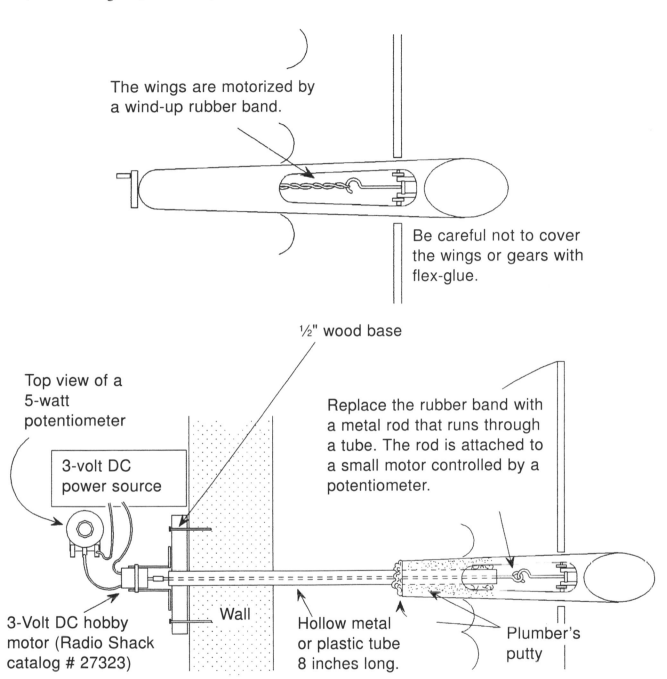

The wings are motorized by a wind-up rubber band.

Be careful not to cover the wings or gears with flex-glue.

½" wood base

Top view of a 5-watt potentiometer

3-volt DC power source

Replace the rubber band with a metal rod that runs through a tube. The rod is attached to a small motor controlled by a potentiometer.

3-Volt DC hobby motor (Radio Shack catalog # 27323)

Wall

Hollow metal or plastic tube 8 inches long.

Plumber's putty

Check to be sure the motor and pot does not get too HOT!

Threatening Object: The Scurrying Rat

As the customers make their way down the hall, a big, hairy rat scurries from a hole in the wall, stops long enough to startle the customers, then turns around and runs back into the hole.

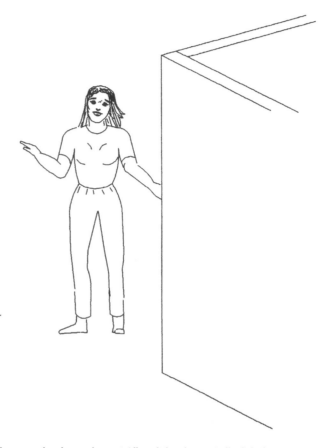

You will need a 4' to 5' length of flat cable. It can be bought at a hardware store as "fishing tape" or as a device that is used to clear drain clogs. It will be a dark color, ¼" wide by ¹⁄₁₆" thick and very flexible in one direction but stiff in the other direction, similar to measuring tape.

This rat can be a rubber rat, or a tail cut off from a raccoon hat. Any flexible scrap of fur will look like a rat when it is quickly moving across the floor.

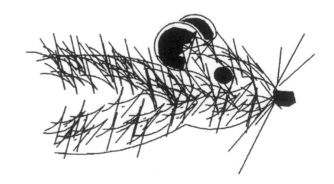

(continued on next page)

(The Scurrying Rat, continued)

Glue a plastic or metal tube to the inside of the rat head from the bottom.

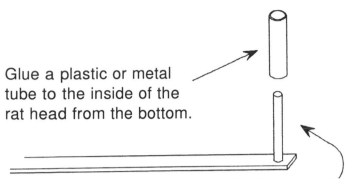

Drill a hole in the cable. Push a nail through the hole and glue it in place, or use a pop-rivet to create a protruding pin. Slide the pin into the tube glued to the bottom of the rat head. The rat will swivel on this to turn around when the cable is pulled back.

Connect the cable to a wood handle, or buy the kind of handle that is normally used to hold files.

Mount a curved PVC pipe against wood with pipe brackets.

The operator will step on the wood base to hold it in place and push, then pull the cable to move the rat.

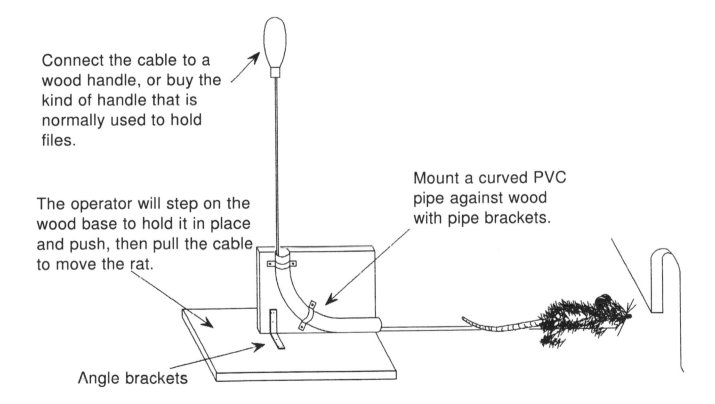

Angle brackets

Threatening Object: The Snake in the Wall

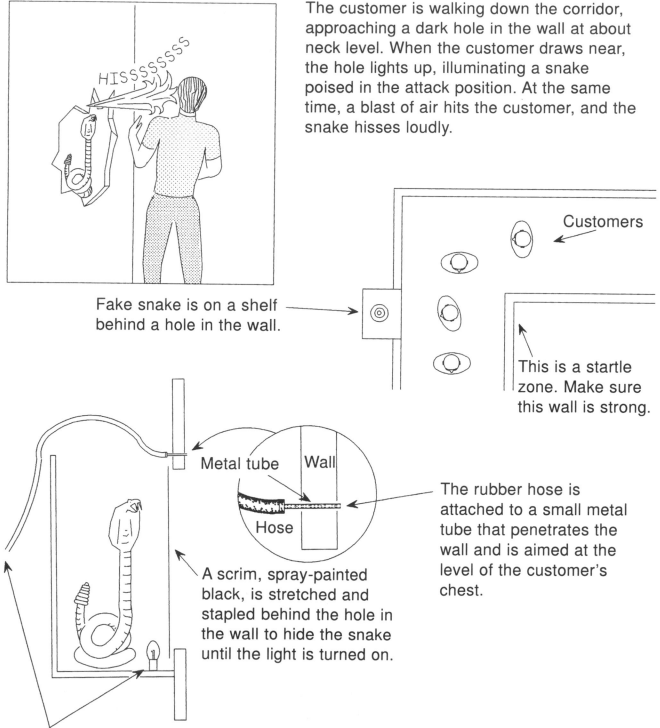

The customer is walking down the corridor, approaching a dark hole in the wall at about neck level. When the customer draws near, the hole lights up, illuminating a snake poised in the attack position. At the same time, a blast of air hits the customer, and the snake hisses loudly.

HISSSSSSSS

Customers

Fake snake is on a shelf behind a hole in the wall.

This is a startle zone. Make sure this wall is strong.

Metal tube Wall

Hose

The rubber hose is attached to a small metal tube that penetrates the wall and is aimed at the level of the customer's chest.

A scrim, spray-painted black, is stretched and stapled behind the hole in the wall to hide the snake until the light is turned on.

The hose is attached to a foot-operated bike pump. The light is a small bright bulb. Both are controlled by an operator who can see the customers through a peephole.

Threatening Object: The Dropping Spiders

The customer is walking down a corridor filled with spiderwebs along the walls and ceilings. Suddenly spiders start dropping from the ceiling in front of the customer's face. Quickly the spiders rise back to the ceiling out of reach. (Do not give the customer a chance to grab the spiders!)

Points where the fake spiders drop down to chest level.

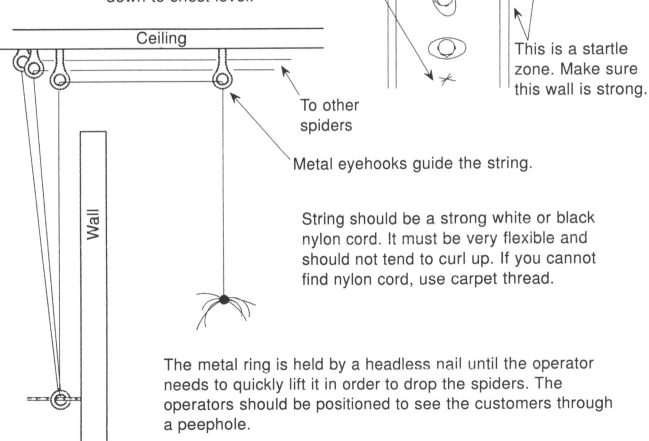

customers

This is a startle zone. Make sure this wall is strong.

Ceiling

To other spiders

Metal eyehooks guide the string.

Wall

String should be a strong white or black nylon cord. It must be very flexible and should not tend to curl up. If you cannot find nylon cord, use carpet thread.

The metal ring is held by a headless nail until the operator needs to quickly lift it in order to drop the spiders. The operators should be positioned to see the customers through a peephole.

4. Props

There are many, many ways to obtain props for your haunted house. Be sure to use refabrication whenever possible. This is a popular trick with prop makers. It means taking something that is close to what you want, reworking it, and painting it to look like the thing you had in mind. For one haunted house, I needed fancy light fixtures to light up the corridors. I priced brass fixtures with glass chimneys and they were $20 to $100 each. Too expensive for the budget I was given. So instead I bought cheap cast-metal floodlight fixtures, plastic clamshell-shaped candy dishes, and tall, fancy, clear plastic champagne glasses. I turned each floodlight fixture upward, cut a plastic champagne glass into a chimney, and attached a clamshell candy dish to the base. Using gold spray paint I gilded the fixture and the base. For a bulb, I used a low-wattage cold flicker light and attached the fancy plastic chimney over the light bulb with epoxy. Even up close, these creations looked like expensive fixtures, but they cost about $4 apiece.

Try to obtain a picture of whatever you are trying to create. Professional special effects technicians do this in order to have a reference for small details and to keep an overview.

Check your local library for books on set design and prop making.

Special Tools

Of course you will need various normal carpentry and craft tools. But there are a few special tools you will also need.

Airbrush: This is a small spray gun that mixes paint and air into a fine mist. It is the only way to apply pigments to a surface without the telltale brushstrokes that hand painting will leave. This is normally a concern only with props that will be seen up close. But props that need a smooth transition from one color to the next will also need the airbrush.

It is not hard to pick up the basic skills. A few practice sessions will get you ready for simple airbrushing. For most simple props the single-action airbrush is adequate. The term "single-action" means that the button controls only the air flow, on or off. The paint flow is controlled by a separate adjustable needle or color control, normally at the front of the airbrush. So there are actually two controls on the single-action airbrush. The button on the double action airbrush controls the air flow and the paint flow. The double-action airbrush can be very expensive ($60 to $150).

I prefer airbrushes with the smallest spray patterns (3/32" or smaller). The smallest spray patterns can paint hair-wide lines for the intricate details like the veins on an eyeball. (If I need to spray large areas there are other tools that can do it, such as the "Preval" spray bottle. This is a reusable glass bottle with an aerosol can which screws to the top of the bottle.) I also like to use a high air-to-paint ratio. This gives me a slow build of pigments. But you will need to clean the airbrush often with this ratio as the extra air tends to dry out the paint in the brush.

Always start and end your stroke *off* your prop. If you start or stop the paint flow while pointing at your prop surface, the paint may splatter. Experiment with various paints, thinning ratios, and air pressures to see what works for you. Also try holding the airbrush at various distances from the surface to be painted.

There are special premixed paints made just for airbrushing, but my favorite paint for this kind of work is water-based acrylic. Water-based paint will not dissolve most surfaces.

Blow dryer: Blow dryers for hair can be used to speed the drying time of paint, water-based glue, latex, etc. I have made a stand that allows me to set the project down in front of the blow dryer and leave the dryer on a low setting. I own several dryers with different features on them. All of them I found in a thrift store. If you only buy one dryer, get one with multiple settings. One of those settings should provide a cold air flow.

Brushes: There are many times when a cheap disposable brush will work just fine — spreading glue, latex or fillers, for example. But most hand painting should be done with the highest-quality brushes you can afford. Keep them clean between colors and you will find that painting will have fewer brush-stroke scars and better pigment control.

Color wheel: Unless you are an expert in color theory, buy this device (don't be cheap on this tool) from an art store. This movable chart tells you which colors are compatible and what happens when you mix a color "hue," "intensity" and "value." (For more on this subject, see Using Color, beginning on page 79.)

Dremel tool: Or the hand grinder, as some call it. This is an all-purpose tool for grinding and shaping small props. It is one of the most prized tools of the model maker. Many different "tips" can be used for different materials. I have found it is worth buying the hands-free attachment that holds the dremel tool to the table. This leaves both hands available to hold and turn the small prop. A drill is a crude substitute because it does not spin the tip as fast, but if you cannot afford to buy the hand grinder, you can just buy the tips and use them with a drill.

Electric oscillating knife: Usually used to carve meats. This device can cut soft and hard foams without tearing the material. Most woodworking tools will work on hard foams.

Heat gun: Similar to a blow dryer, but much more powerful. It is used to heat up and shape plastics. Fake ironwork can be made this way by bending PVC water pipe. Many shapes can be made by hand with vacuum-form plastics. Be sure to use welder's gloves to protect your hands. Large plastic sheets can be heated up in the kitchen oven. Lay aluminum foil down first to protect the inside of the oven.

Hot glue gun: This has become extremely popular in the last few years as a craft tool. The glue becomes strongly cohesive when heated to its melting point and cures to maximum strength as soon as it cools. Some stores carry more than one kind of glue stick. There are dozens of formulas for different purposes. The all-purpose hot glue stick is not strong, but it will stick to almost anything, dries quickly, and is waterproof and flexible. You can make small castings with hot glue, or use the string of glue to make fake carvings in props. I decorated an old haunted house organ by using the hot glue gun to create lines and circles on the surface. When it was dry, I painted the organ with a wood grain technique (see pages 77–78), then covered it in several thin layers of watered down flex-glue. When it was finished the hot glue designs looked like intricate carving. The flex-glue gave it a deep, wet, lacquered look.

Temporary wood structures can be held quite well with hot glue. I also have hung decorations on the walls with hot glue. It is easy to pull the glue off later without too much harm to the wall surface. In short, the hot glue gun is an indispensable fastening device and should be used whenever possible. Look for it in hardware, craft and hobby stores.

Nibbling tool: Cuts light-gauge sheet metal or plastic. A hole is drilled or punched into the sheet, and the head of the nibbler is inserted into the hole. This hand-held device is then squeezed and moved around to cut square or triangular holes and channels. These can be bought from Radio Shack and other stores that sell electrical tools.

Nail gun or brad gun: If you will be constructing wood props that will not be torn apart completely, the pneumatic nail gun will take a lot of the work and time out of the project. Don't bother with the electric guns, which are not powerful enough. You will need an air compressor with at least 90 PSI capability. By turning up the pressure, the nails can be sunk into the wood just below the surface. This makes sanding much easier.

Opaque projector: This special projector will take a normal photograph or hand-drawn image and project it on to a wall. The drawing (11" × 8½" or smaller) is placed under the projector. A light bulb illuminates the drawing, and a mirror reflects the image through the lens onto the wall. This way a complicated background scene can be duplicated by roughly tracing the projected image onto the wall. Once the basic lines are drawn, you can turn off the projector and use the lines as a guide to painting. These projectors can be bought at art, hobby, craft and toy stores. Definitely shop around because the price will vary considerably.

Popsicle sticks: Wood popsicle sticks can be bought cheaply from craft stores. These are used as disposable mixing sticks.

Staple gun: Use a staple gun for attaching door skins or ²⁄₁₆" plywood sheets to wood frames. Large, heavy props can be simulated with this technique. Staple guns are great for tacking cloth to wood. Get the most powerful gun you can afford. The cheaper ones tend not to have the power to sink the staple properly.

Special Materials

Always shop around for the best prices; large home improvement stores have better prices, but small hardware stores have better selection. Always read the labels on materials. You will be surprised to find the same product sold under different names for different purposes. Depending on the intended use of the product it will be sold at greatly varying prices.

I priced natural latex rubber at $10 an ounce from makeup suppliers. The product sold for mold making cost $14 for a 16-ounce container. And finally I found natural latex rubber at $7 for a 16-ounce container. It was sold as a glue to adhere rugs to the floor.

Acrylic monomers and polymers: These are two-part acrylics (a liquid plus a powder) used by dentists for false teeth and gums or by beauticians for fingernails. A dental supply house will carry them, but they will be cheaper from beauty supply stores. They can be used as cement on fiberglass and some plastic props. Many prop makers use them to glue control cables to the puppet armatures for animated props. For cementing it will not matter which color you use, but clear or white is what I recommend. They will harden very quickly, so plan on a fast mix and application time. The liquid is slightly toxic, so you should wear rubber gloves.

Aluminum flashing: A soft, pliable sheet metal that roofers use to cover gutters. It can be soldered or riveted and cut with tin snips. It can be obtained at any hardware store.

Aviary wire: A version of chicken wire with a finer mesh. Used by prop makers to make small frames to support, reinforce, and sculpt papier-mâché with better detail than can be had using chicken wire. Look in the phone book for hardware or pet supply stores.

Bondo: (Dynatton/Bondo Corp. trade name): A plastic body filler used in auto body and fender repair. Look for it at hardware and auto supply stores.

Caulking sealant: Similar to flex-glue (see next page), but much thicker and more expensive. I use the clear type (brand name Climacel) to fake paintings by brushing it

onto framed posters and lithographs. It can be obtained at hardware stores, or contact Macklanburg-Duncan, 4041 N. Santa Fe, Oklahoma City, Oklahoma 73118.

Celastic: Used as a substitute for papier-mâché. It dries faster and is much more fire resistant. It resembles strips of canvas and is dipped into acetone in a bucket to make it workable. Check the phone book for theater supply companies.

Contact cement: Bonding for almost any surface, including leather and cloth. The solvents in this glue may attack some surfaces. Large quantities may be bought cheaply as a tile and floor cement. Remember that any product that an industry uses in large quantities tends to be cheaper. If you were to buy contact cement from a craft store it would be more expensive because hobbyists use less of the product than carpenters do in their projects.

Cyanoacrylate (Super Glue, gap filler, etc.): This is a very fast-drying glue that becomes hard and brittle almost instantly. It can be obtained at hardware or hobby stores or even supermarkets (in very small, relatively expensive quantities). Use it for small decorations or repairs of small items that need a high tensile strength but not a high torque strength. There is a new line of flexible glues of this type. When they dry they have much greater holding power because of their higher torque strength. Cyanoacrylate will work on wood, metal, china and ceramics, and hard plastics. The kind used for fingernail repair is non-toxic in small quantities. Cyanoacrylate can be debonded with nail polish remover (acetone).

I once had a problem with sticking horns to my forehead. The horns were just too heavy for the prosthetic adhesive I had. So I used a small amount of fingernail repair glue. The horns held to my skin perfectly. To remove them I used a debonding agent and carefully peeled them off. I am not recommending this (it was a little painful), but it was the only way I could get the horns to stay on. After this experience I made the horns smaller to make them lighter.

Detergent: Used by prop makers as a paint additive and cleanser. Small amounts added to paint reduce surface tension, allowing the color to flow. Larger quantities reduce the sticking ability of paint, allowing for easier clean-up. This can be liquid dishwashing or laundry detergent, available at any supermarket. Buy a brand with no perfumes or colors.

Door skins: Very thin panel wood, used to simulate thick wood structures by stapling to wood frames. Large sheets (4' × 8') can be used to make non-structural walls for background sets. Look for them at hardware stores and lumberyards.

Duct tape: A wide, cloth-backed tape, usually gray but available in other colors. Used for a variety of tape needs; obtain at any hardware store. Get black for general purpose, or white if the tape is to be painted.

Durham's Rockhard Water Putty (Donald Durham Co. trade name): This water-mixed putty is used for filling wide gaps in wood. It can also be used as a casting material or as a hard skin on foam props. It can be found at any hardware store.

Dye: Liquid pigments that penetrate the fiber of the surface to be colored. Bleaching can reverse the dyeing process. Remember that unlike paint a light colored dye will not cover a dark colored dye.

Epoxy (five-minute): This two-part glue also comes in a ten-minute version for longer working times. It dries crystal-clear, which makes it a good transparent hard skin for props like eyeballs. This kind of epoxy will glue wood, metal, china and ceramics.

Epoxy paste: This two-part epoxy is similar to epoxy putty (see below), but the resulting mixture is much more pliable, which makes it easier to spread. Many brands can be found at most hardware stores. This will glue wood, metal, china, ceramics and hard plastics.

Epoxy putty or plumber's putty: A very tenacious, hard-drying putty. In propmaking it is usually used as a material for sculpting small items that take a lot of abuse. I have used it to fill in and hand-shape molding corners. It is available at most hardware stores, or by contacting the Martin Carboni Co., Santa Barbara, California, (805) 628-0465, and asking for the name brand Hand Workable Epoxy Putty.

Falcon Foam (Falcon Foam Plastics, Inc., trade name): An expanded polystyrene. Prop makers use it for fake stone and also as a sculpting material. Can be found at marine supply houses, along with Styrofoam (see pages 75–76).

Flex-glue: A milky white adhesive made of polyvinyl acetate (PVA) that remains flexible and crystal-clear when dry. Used commercially as a bookbinding adhesive. Used by prop makers as a texturing medium as well as an adhesive and a glaze to replicate varnish. It can be colored with shoe polish or other tinting agents. It can also be used as an embedding agent to apply decorations to various surfaces and make them look like an integral part of the surface. For example, I glued plastic spiders and other decorations to a grandfather clock, covered it with many layers of flex-glue, and painted it to look like wood. The result was the appearance of intricate wood carvings. Flex-glue can be obtained in gallon quantities by contacting Spectra Dynamics, Albuquerque, New Mexico, (505) 843-7202. The brand name is Phlexglu.

Foliage flameproofing and preserving: A green paint based in neoprene rubber, used as a flameproofing agent for natural plants used in sets. It also keeps the leaves fresh by preventing drying through evaporation. Contact California Flameproofing, Pasadena, California, (213) 681-6773. The product is listed under the name No. 57 Green.

Friendly Plastic: This amazing product looks like normal plastic but can be softened in hot water and shaped with your hands like putty. It can be bought at craft and hobby stores.

Glue cloth: This is a molding technique in which repeated coatings of cloth strips soaked in glue are placed over a wire form. The process is the same as papier-mâché, except that cloth is used instead of paper. Large props (such as rock formations) can be made by soaking old bedsheets in liquid starch and shaping them on chicken wire and wood frames.

Hot glue: See "hot glue gun" under Special Tools, pages 70–71.

Latex rubber: A liquid rubber that dries in the air to form a flexible coating. Used for making soft "skins" on rigid forms, and for making flexible castings from plaster molds. It can be tinted to look like skin. Always tint it lighter than is needed; as it dries the color becomes much darker. It can be bought from makeup distributors already tinted, but I buy a product called "Fiber-Loc" (from ETI, Fields Landing, CA 95537)

which is used to glue rugs to the floor. Read the ingredient list on the canister. You will find it is like natural latex that is sold for mold casting but is *much* cheaper. It is mixed with ammonia to thin the latex, but it can be further thinned with purified water.

Miscellaneous materials: Thrift stores are a wonderful source of props and devices. For example, for a few dollars I have bought thrift-store rotisserie motors that are perfect for slow-moving motorized effects (rotisserie motors are usually used to turn meat over a barbecue). It is worth your time to constantly check thrift stores for equipment and materials before buying them new.

Paint: Paint is actually a colored powder that is glued to a surface. The three parts of paint are the *pigment*, which is the color; the *binder*, which is the "glue"; and the *vehicle*, which is the thinner that keeps the glue from setting until the vehicle has evaporated.

Care must be taken to find the right binder for the surface to be painted, and the right vehicle to "thin" the glue. For example, few watercolors will adhere to metal or glass. The weak binder in children's paint will not adhere to these nonporous surfaces. Some binders that will stick to a surface may not flex the same way as the surface. When a nonflexible binder is used on a surface that is flexible, the paint will crack and peel off. The vehicle must be compatible with the binder, and some vehicles will attack the surface. For instance, an oil-based paint will attack many rubber surfaces. Always read the labels on the paint you intend to use, and experiment on scrap material.

Paints will dry glossy, semi-glossy or flat. Glossy is shiny, while flat will absorb the shine. I prefer flat colors in general. If I need a glossy surface I usually apply a clear coat such as acrylic or flex-glue after the paint has dried. There is also a choice of opaque or translucent color. Translucence will allow the prop maker to layer colors — for instance, to mimic the way you can see blue veins under skin.

Pilot ink: This ink is used to refill the giant Pilot felt tip pen. The ink is similar to the kind used in "permanent" markers. It comes in black, blue, red, brown, and green. (Not yellow, unfortunately.) It will stick to almost any surface and dries instantly. It is made in screw-top bottles and can be bought from stationery stores or office supply houses. I use small paintbrushes to apply it.

Pipe wire: A black small-diameter metal wire similar to the wire used for clothes hangers. Used for a variety of binding and hanging needs.

Plastic and fiberglass rods, tubes, sheets, films, resins: Used for various construction needs. Look in your local phone directory, or contact Cadillac Plastics, 1125 Vanowen St., North Hollywood, California 91605-6318, (818) 980-0840, or S & W Plastics at 1200 Wanmaker Avenue, Ontario, California 91761, (909) 988-5403.

Plastic body filler: Used as a fiberglass putty by prop makers; can also be used for molding and adhesive purposes. Hardware stores and auto supply stores should carry it.

Plastic cement: Used to connect plastic parts. It fuses plastic together chemically. I use the type for bonding PVC pipes; it is obtained at hardware stores. There are also many new formulas sold at hobby shops. If you mix this cement with spare parts from plastic models, the model parts will dissolve. The resulting mixture is a plastic putty that you can use to fill gaps in plastic, or shape to form small plastic parts.

Scrim: This is a special cloth with a wide open-weave pattern. If scrim is draped or stretched before a dark area and a light source is used on the customer's side, the scrim appears solid. If a light is used on the opposite side the scrim becomes transparent. Go to a school drama department and ask to see this stuff. Once you have a good idea of what it looks like you may be able to find similar cloth in a sewing supply store, but if you can afford it, buy the scrim from a theatrical supply house. It will cost several dollars per square foot. Ask for remnants of white-colored "shark's tooth" scrim.

Silicone rubber adhesive: Waterproof (most other adhesives are *not* able to withstand constant exposure to water) and flexible glue for glass, metal, and ceramics. Dries clear. This adhesive can be bought from hardware stores.

Skin-Flex series: These are extremely stretchable, skinlike materials that can be bought from special effects supply distributors. The Skin-Flex series includes Skin-Flex III brushable liquid, primer paints and pigments. Other products for flexible skins are "BJB LS-60" elastomer and "BJB LS-61" elastomer.

If you cannot find a special effects supplier near you call Burman Industries at (818) 782-9833, or write to them at 14141 Covello Street, Suite 6-A, Van Nuys, California 91405.

Spray adhesive: Found at hardware stores or art and craft supply stores. I have found that the expensive brand name 3M Super 77 construction (not craft) spray adhesive is worth the extra cost. Produced by the 3M Company, it is a form of contact cement and can be used to glue most surfaces.

Styrofoam (Dow Chemical trade name):

Expanded styrene, not urethane. The two are different, though common usage has confused the two. Look in marine supply stores for Styrofoam.

Tinting agents: Leather dyes, fabric and textile dyes, lamp dips and glass stains can be used as tinting agents. Aluminum powders, bronzing powders, and graphite can be used alone or with other dyes to produce metal finishes. All these can be found at paint, craft, and hardware stores. Food coloring and aniline dyes (such as Rit) can be obtained at grocery stores. Use a tinting agent with a binding agent such as flex-glue to create your own paint. Remember that flex-glue looks milky white before it dries. You may have to experiment with the tinting to get the shade you want when it dries.

Trickline: A black venetian blind cord. Used for any job that requires a strong, small-diameter rope.

Upson board: Layers of paper are pressed and glued to create this woodlike sheet. It can be easily curved and cut with a utility knife. It is really a thick cardboard that will warp if not painted lightly.

Urethane foam: This material can be either hard or flexible in form. Hard urethane can be carved. Flexible urethane is used for padding and can be found at upholstery shops in large quantities.

Surface Treatments and Finishes

Cover props with flex-glue or latex rubber for a flexible skin. You can first add pigment to the flex-glue or latex if you like, then brush it or spray it on, depending on the results you need. If your budget will allow it, you can use professional surface treatments like the Skin-Flex products (see under Special Materials).

Use epoxy paste, Bondo, fiberglass or Durham's Rockhard Water Putty for a hard skin over hard foam. Mix the compounds as described in their instructions, spread the mix with a spatula or brush (depending on the thickness of the mixture). When dry, sand smooth and paint. Sometimes hard foam props need only a skin of white glue (like Elmer's) and paint. You will need to experiment with scrap as some of these skins may work better than others on a particular surface. The Rockhard Water Putty will work on most hard surfaces and is inexpensive.

Painting soft foam and rubber surfaces can be a real headache for the inexperienced prop maker. The paint will crack or rub off and sometimes dissolve the surface, making a real mess. There are professional paints specially formulated for the special effects industry, but these can be very expensive. I suggest you try the following methods. They were first used 30 years ago, and because the technology is old, they tend to be much cheaper; yet the results can be very good if the methods are used correctly. (If you are interested in professional paints, contact a special effects supply company.)

The first method is to make your own paint by mixing a rubber glue with pigments. Rubber cement is the most common binder for this technique.

Dilute the thick glue with a rubber cement thinner such as Bestine from art stores or xylol (also called xylene), mineral spirits or VM&P Naphtha from a hardware store. I prefer Bestine or xylol, but these are both toxic chemicals. Use rubber gloves and a respirator and work in a well-ventilated area. The pigments used could be oil paint or water-based acrylics. You can also use a "universal pigment" from art stores. When creating your homemade paint, you may need to use white pigment first, then add color. This gives the color a foundation to work on. Otherwise the paint may be too translucent.

If you are airbrushing the paint, use an external mixing brush. Try setting your compressor up to 60 PSI with an airbrush tip that will give you the widest opening to help prevent clogging. The caustic nature of the thinners may damage the plastic parts, so be sure to clean your airbrush thoroughly when done.

The second method is easier on your airbrush because you can use water-based acrylic without any glue mixed into the paint. For large foam or rubber props that don't need to stretch a great deal, spray the surface with a light coat of a high-quality, fine-mist spray adhesive like Super 77 by the 3M Company. Once it has had a little time to dry, you can airbrush or hand-paint the prop with any kind of paint that will not attack the glue. The paint will stick to the adhesive, and the adhesive will stick to the prop.

For highly stretchable props like rubber latex masks, you will need to use a special primer before painting. Make the primer by thinning any kind of high-tack, stretchable glue. Then apply it to the prop with a sponge. You can use spirit gum thinned with spirit gum remover, or hairpiece glue, or prosthetic glue (a medical product for attaching rubber prostheses).

The best is a product called "Pros-aide." The Pros-aide glue can be thinned with water. A 50/50 blend is a good general mix of Pros-aide to water. After the Pros-aide has dried, it will remain tacky. Do a

base coat of one color (such as white) by mixing the Pros-aide with water and water-based pigments. Sponge the mix onto the prop. When this is dry you can airbrush the prop with acrylic paint. The tackiness should be gone by the time you have finished airbrushing. But if the prop is still tacky after the paint is dry, pat on some translucent makeup powder. Carefully blow or brush off the excess powder. This same method is used to take the tackiness out of face makeup.

To make a surface look like wood grains, you will need a black, light tan, or whitish-yellow base coat and a brown top coat. Buy a "combing tool" from a craft store, or make one by cutting a cardboard square and cutting v-shaped notches to produce a giant "comb" with varying sized teeth. (See illustration on page 78.) Paint the prop with the base coat. Let it dry. Then paint with the top coat. While the top coat is still wet, rake the prop firmly with the comb. This will produce streaks, allowing the base coat to show through. Soften the effect by pulling the bristles of a wide, dry paintbrush along the streaks, following the same direction. Wipe the brush with a paper towel after each pass to keep it dry.

You can also use a heart wood graining tool, a device that looks like a quarter round rubber stamp with a handle. The pattern on the stamp produces a broad-ringed wood grain when drawn through the wet top coat. By rocking the tool, you can vary the grain pattern. The consistency of the top coat should be easy to brush. If the paint is too stiff, stir in a few drops of thinner or water, depending on the chemical base of the paint.

Once you have your wood grain established, you may want to reproduce an antique effect by "flyspecking." Flyspecks are the little dark spots on older objects. Thin a

Wood Grain Painting Technique

This square represents the wall or prop that is to be painted to resemble a wood grain surface.

First paint the subject with a base of dark brown, black, or tan/yellow. Let it dry thoroughly.

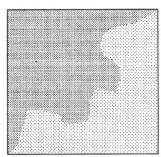

Then paint over with a coat of brown or dark cherry red. You may want to do this in patches because you will need to work the top coat before it dries.

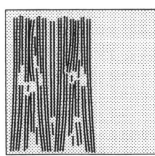

Rake the top coat with a cardboard "comb" or a rat-tail hair brush to create streaks like the grain in wood.

Cardboard cut into a comb.

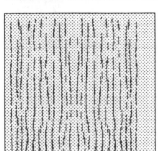

Soften the lines with a dry, wide paintbrush. Brush the lines in the same direction that the comb was used. Once the paint has dried, you might coat the object with a thin skin of flex-glue for a varnished look.

small amount of a black paint, then dip an old toothbrush in the thinned paint and tap off the excess on a paper towel. Hold the brush with bristles down about 6" above the project's surface. Run your thumb across the bristles while moving your hand to release a fine spatter of dots.

"Scrumbling," or "wet blending," is the softening of the edges of two adjacent colors so that they blend. It is done with a clean brush while the colors are still wet. This technique is used to create highlight or shadow or to create the illusion of a rounded surface. (See illustration on page 80.)

"Lining" is used to create the illusion of molding on a flat surface. You will need two others to help with this, and a straight stick. While the two helpers hold the stick just above the surface to be painted, the painter runs a small brush along the stick, just as one might draw a line on paper with a straightedge. But the stick must not touch the surface or the paint will work its way under and splotch the line. Use a lighter shade on top of the line and a darker shade on the bottom of the line to create the illusion of a protruding edge. (See illustration on page 81.)

You can recreate stone surfaces, such as granite or marble, with paint techniques as well. (See illustration on page 82.) Finished "stone" looks good for walls, mantles, tombstones and other props. For granite, coat the object with a white base and let it dry. Then swirl together (don't mix thoroughly or blend) black and white top coat paints in a figure-eight pattern. Pat a sponge, preferably a natural sea sponge (better texture effects), into the swirled colors and blot the excess on a paper towel. Gently pat the paint onto the surface of your project in several random areas, trying not to create an obvious pattern. Keep the sponge straight up and down. To prevent streaking, don't move it

while it is on the surface; always lift the sponge to move to another area.

For marble, start the same way you did for granite, but before the top coats dry, drag a wet feather through the paint in wavy, random lines to simulate the veins in marble. Then, dip the feather into a thinned amount of the base coat you used and "draw" more random lines.

Stencils and stamps can be used to repeat patterns on a surface. Stencils can be bought or cut from cardboard, metal or wax paper. Spraying or dabbing the paint with a sponge works better than brushing. Hard brushing may work the paint under the stencil. Stamps can be cut from sponge or other foam products. Spray or brush the paint onto the stamp. For both stamping and stencil work, apply the paint sparingly to prevent dripping or smudging.

Using Color

Color communicates a great deal of information. A color scheme is a combination of hues, greys, shades, translucent tints and highlights. Because of the way the eye and brain work to interpret color information, placing colors next to each other will affect how they both look. Color information can suggest emotion, movement, temperature, time of day and weather. Colors can depict stages of decay and age, and there are groups of colors that are found under particular conditions. Light conditions such as twilight have a great deal of the ultraviolet spectrum, but not much of the normal spectrum. Consequently, at twilight the fluorescent pigments in flowers tend to look bright, but colors from the middle of the spectrum will wash out to a dull grey.

Scrumbling Technique

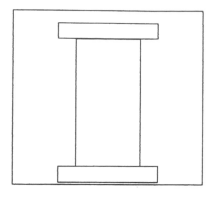

This square represents a wall with a round pedestal painted on it. Here the pedestal looks flat because there is no shading work done yet.

Make sure these lines are dry before doing the next few steps.

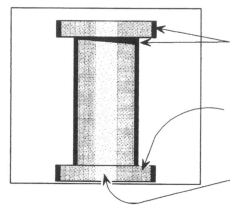

Black paint is applied.
Note the dark shadow under the pedestal's protruding lip.

Dark grey paint is applied.

Light grey paint is applied.

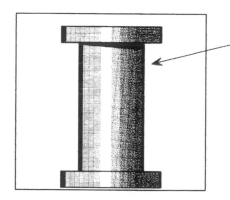

Before the paint dries, take a clean brush and "smudge" the harsh transition lines where the darker and lighter paints meet. Keep cleaning your brush as you work around the entire painting. Do not mix your strokes: use either up-and-down or left-and-right strokes.

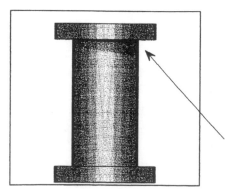

The finished product will be a smoother change from one color to the next. This will create the illusion of a cylinder with three-dimensional depth.

Work the shadow under the pedestal's protruding lip to soften it.

Lining Technique

This square represents a wall that will be painted to look like wood wainscoting and molding, a woodwork style that was popular in Victorian homes. (This same technique can be used to paint large windowpanes and various wood carvings.)

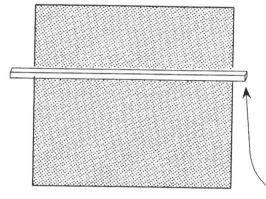

Lay down the base color in a cherrywood red, walnut or some other wood color. You could flyspeck dark color for texture. Then have two helpers hold a straight stick in the place where you want to draw your line, slightly off the surface.

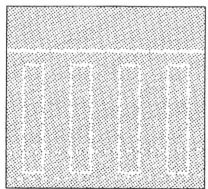

Using the same base paint but with white added to it, drag a paintbrush along the stick to paint light-colored lines. These lines will represent areas of carved wood that catch the light.

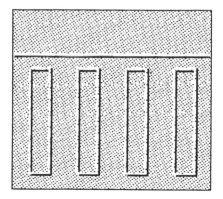

Using the same base paint but with black added to it, drag a paintbrush along the stick to paint dark-colored lines. These lines will represent areas of carved wood that block the light. As always you should work from color pictures of real examples.

Rock Wall Painting Technique

This square represents the wall or prop that is to be painted to resemble a rock structure.

First mix white and black paint to make a medium gray. Paint the wall with a sprayer, brush or roller.

Now with white, very light gray or black paint, brush the outlines of the rocks. In this example we are using white paint to represent the mortar that would be used to hold the rocks together.

Take the gray that was used as the base and add black to make a dark gray mix. Using a natural sponge or a crumbled newspaper, lightly blot patches of dark areas to represent the shade from light blocked by the protrusions of the rock.

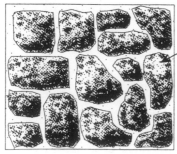

Mix the rest of the gray base paint with white to make a very light gray. Lightly blot patches of bright areas opposite the dark areas to represent the protrusions that would catch more light than the rest of the rock.

Keep in mind the effects of light on your props and sets. A wallpaper design with red flowers and green leaves on a white background will change drastically under red light. The red light will bounce off the white paper to the eyes, and the red flowers will also bounce red light to the eyes. Meanwhile, the green leaves will tend to absorb all colors except green, so when a red light hits the green pigments it will be absorbed and will not bounce any light back to the eyes. Thus the flowers will disappear and the leaves will turn black.

I will attempt to give you a basic understanding of color theory and mixing, but you should start by copying color schemes from pictures, movies, and careful observation of your world around you.

Variables in Color

Hue distinguishes blue from red, yellow from blue, etc. A degree of black or white is called admixture. Adding black to orange will create the color brown. When color pigments are mixed together, the eye interprets it as one new color. Yellow and blue pigments mixed together will appear green to the eye. The spectrum of colors can be arranged in a circular pattern called a color wheel, on which it is easy to see how the colors relate to one another. (See illustration on page 85.) Colors in the red and yellow family are considered warm, and colors in the blue family are considered cool. The wheel is not cut in half for warm and cool colors; warm colors make up two-thirds of the wheel.

The primary colors are red, yellow and blue. These three can be combined to create all the other colors on the wheel. The secondary colors are orange, which is red and yellow mixed evenly; green, which is yellow and blue mixed evenly; and purple, which is red and blue mixed evenly. In between the secondary and primary colors are various shades of hue. Thus the wheel is divided into three groups with the primary colors of red, blue and yellow as the dividing lines. The three color groups are the orange, purple and green.

Black is a combination of red, blue and yellow pigments that absorbs all colors of light, reflecting no color back to the eyes. Now it gets a little confusing: Normal light comes in three colors, red, blue and green. When pigments reflect all three colors of light at the same time, the eye interprets the mix as white. When pigments reflect green and blue light together, the eye interprets the mix as yellow. Thus paint pigments *subtract* one or more of the colors from the combined color spectrum.

Adding black to a color is called greying and will make the color seem warmer, richer, slower, quieter, heavier. It will make a color seem farther away from the viewer when it is up close, and will create the illusion of a more opaque hue. Adding white to a color is called pastelling and will make the color look faster, cooler, lighter, louder. It will make a color seem more distant when it is set far from the viewer, and will create the illusion of a more translucent hue. If both white and black are added to a color they will not cancel each other out; instead, they will create a muddy color that can become very busy. But mixing unequal amounts of black and white with a color can add subtle complexity.

Color Mixing

Pairs of colors that produce black when mixed together are sometimes called "complementaries." Usually these pairs consist of a primary color and the opposite secondary color, such as yellow and purple. Technically, if you were to mix the three primary colors together evenly, you would produce black, but pure primary colors are almost impossible to buy. For example, a jar marked primary yellow will have some white mixed into it. Mixing this contaminated yellow with red and blue would result in a muddy grey color. When you are mixing secondary and primary colors, try to think of the secondary colors in terms of their primary components. For example, if you mix a quart of blue with a quart of orange, you have actually mixed two pints of blue with one pint of red and one pint of yellow. So out of the four pints you have mixed one red, one yellow, and one blue — resulting in three pints of black — plus one pint of blue. The end product is four pints of very dark blue.

The primary colors are rarely used as they are. They are too striking and can become visually irritating. Often colors are visually controlled by adding a small amount of another color. Examples are Chinese red (red with a little yellow), blue-green (blue with a little yellow), and yellow-green (yellow with a little blue). This can sometimes make it quite difficult to make existing colors or create specific colors. Suppose you are trying to mix a yellow-green to paint leaves on a tree, and you mix a pint of yellow that has been contaminated with a drop of red into a pint of green. The single drop of red will combine with a drop of blue and a drop of yellow that are already in the green. This would result in three drops of black, which would be quite noticeable in the final quart of paint. This contamination problem can be difficult to deal with for props viewed by a close-up camera. Fortunately, in your haunted house your props will probably not be subjected to this kind of scrutiny. Nevertheless, you should always strive for the best result you can get each step of the way. Little imperfections here and there can add up to a ridiculously unconvincing prop if care is not taken.

Shade and Highlights

Depressions and protrusions will catch the light and reflect it differently. Depressions in a prop, such as the space between the ribs on a corpse, will appear darker; protrusions such as cheekbones will appear lighter. Sometimes the pigments on skin will cluster or be less dense due to the skin being stretched or bunched. The knuckles of the hand are darker when the hand is relaxed. The cheeks appear lighter when a person is whistling because the skin is pulled taut.

To create the effects of depressions and protrusions, you will need a base color, a highlight, and a shade. The method is simple: After you have mixed the chosen color for your prop, divide the paint into one large and two smaller portions. The large amount will be the base paint and the two smaller portions will be the highlight and the shade. You can make the shade by simply mixing the base paint with a small amount of black, and the highlight by mixing the base with a small amount of white. However, a better result would come from using the darker and lighter colors that were used to mix the paint. For example, if the base paint is orange, you can make the shade by mixing the base orange with red and a little black. The highlight would be the base orange plus yellow and a little white.

Remember that props like a severed head should be painted in layered colors to

Color Wheel

All colors can be made by mixing
red, yellow, blue and white.

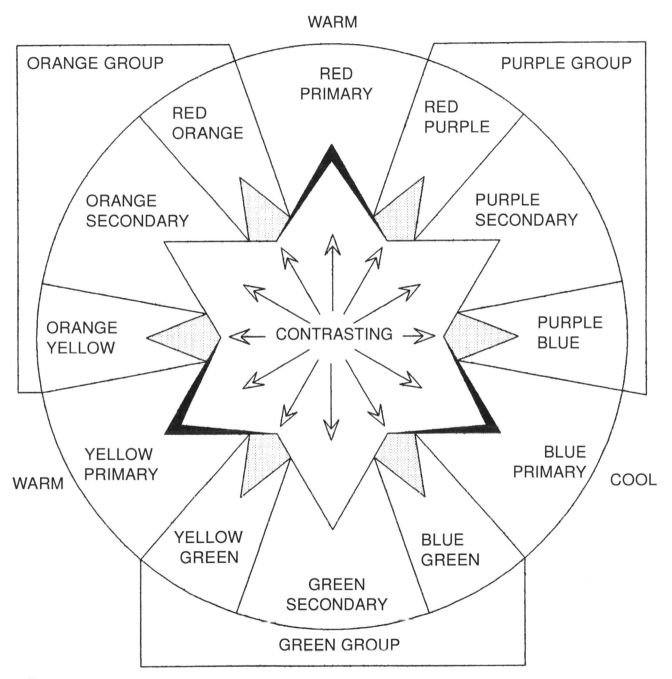

Red + Yellow + Blue = Black
White + Black = Grey
Orange + Black = Brown

create a translucent effect. Skin is not just a peach, brown, yellow or red color. Under the skin are purple and green tones, with more red in fleshy areas and white in bony areas. Paint the prop with hints of these colors, then cover with the appropriate skin color, using thinned paint so that the undercolors show through.

Contrasting and Harmonious Colors

Colors contrast when they lie directly opposite each other on the color wheel. Green and red, yellow and purple, orange and blue are contrasting colors.

Colors are in harmony when they are from the same color group. Green, yellow-green and yellow would be good for painting a reptilian monster mask. You could paint the folds and deep lines of the skin green, the scales yellow-green, and the horns or teeth yellow.

To highlight details, such as the lips and inside of the mouth and ears, a contrasting color could be used. If we look at the direct opposite of the chosen color scheme we find red-purple is the contrasting color. Maybe this creates too harsh a contrast. Instead, you could pick a color that is not directly in contrast with the chosen scheme, such as red or purple. Purple is a cooler color and is less of a contrast than the warmer color of red. You might think that orange is even closer to the color scheme and would be less of a contrast to the yellow, but it will contrast sharply with the green and result in a clashing effect.

Paying attention to the color wheel is a simple but effective way to keep elements in balance when designing a color scheme.

Some Basic Props

Making a Corpse

Kits for making a life-sized rotting human corpse can be bought from special effects supply companies. These kits include latex or plastic parts that must be assembled and airbrushed. Such kits and even pre-assembled props will cost between $200 and $1000. I will describe a method for making a very convincing life-sized corpse that will cost only around $30.

You will first need to buy a cheap plastic "Lab Skeleton" sold at novelty stores. You can also buy these lab skeletons at costume shops and drug stores in October. I bought mine from a chain called "Pick and Save" for only $10. They are made in China for Halloween distribution. These toys are hollow plastic and they look ridiculous, but they are close enough to the size and shape of a realistic skeleton to work with a little refabrication.

First assemble the skeleton. Use hard urethane foam and contact glue to fill out the stomach area. Shape the foam with a rasp and sandpaper. Don't make it protrude; remember the corpse is supposed to have lost much fat as it aged. It will look better to make the stomach sink into the body.

Spray a small section of the prop with a good-quality contact glue like 3M Super 77 aerosol adhesive. Rip sections from white paper towels and spread them evenly on the sprayed section of the plastic. Push the paper towels into the depressions and smooth over protrusions. As you finish one area, spray another with the adhesive and resume the paper towel procedure.

You should tear the paper so that there are no straight lines; creating paper sections with erratic edges will help to blend the surface. Otherwise the straight edges of the paper will show up as lines on the finished project. Don't worry if some of the paper hangs off the plastic. The spray glue is just to help hold the paper in place for the next step.

Mix about one cup of flex-glue with one cup of water. Tint the mix with water-based paint. Various color schemes can be used, such as peach-blue or light tan. Remember that when the flex-glue dries it will be a darker shade.

Use a paintbrush to apply layers of the mix to the paper. It will soak in and bind the paper into a skinlike shell very much like papier-mâché.

When you have paper-toweled and painted the whole front side, let the prop dry, then turn it over and do the back the same way.

Some paper soaked in the mix can be used as a putty to create shriveled ears and a belly button for realism. Once the paper-and-glue mix has completely dried, it will look like shriveled and aged skin on the plastic skeleton.

Now you will need to airbrush the dark regions such as the eye sockets and the depressions between the ribs. If you can obtain colored pictures of mummies or other aged bodies it will help you in the process.

Next, with a second color such as dark brown, lightly spray the entire prop, using water-based paint. This will create a layered, translucent look to the "skin." Keep the airbrush two or three feet away and spray just enough to see the second color.

Once this coat is dry, cut the skin from the skull's mouth area with a razor blade or hobby knife. Color the dark regions between the teeth and the gum line with black paint. Paint the teeth white, but allow the dark areas to show.

Mix some flex-glue with a small amount of yellow food coloring. Paint this onto the teeth to create a deep, aged stain.

Finally, spray adhesive to the head and layer on some white or gray hair. Don't make a full head of hair, just enough to suggest that the head had hair at one time. Fake hair can be bought from beauty supply stores. It is used to add extensions to hair for styling. It comes in a three-foot-long bundle and only costs about $5. It is great for such projects because it comes in a variety of colors and is much cheaper than wigs. In October many beauty supply stores will also stock fantasy colors such as white and green.

If you cannot find the hair extensions or you just want to keep the project simple, buy an old wig from a thrift store. You may be able to color the wig white with one of the temporary hair colors that are sold around October.

You might pop some homemade eyes (see Eyeball Appetizer, page 90) into the skull. If you do this at the beginning of the process you will need to cover the front of the eyes with a mold release such as car wax. Build eyelids over the eyes with the paper-and-glue mix. Don't forget to cover the eyes with masking tape before spraying the prop with paint. The car wax will help keep glue and paint from sticking to the front of the eyes. Once the prop is done, clean the wax off the eyes with a cloth.

Body Forms

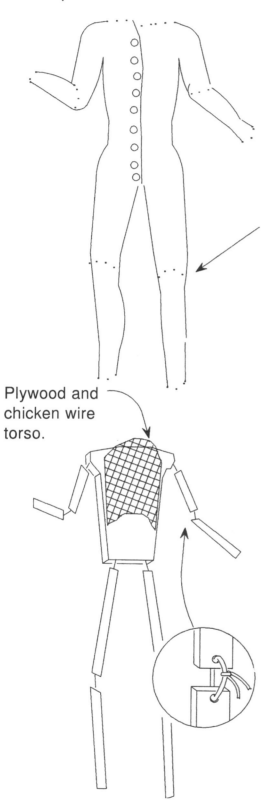

Plywood and chicken wire torso.

Mannequins make good bodies but can be hard to find. Thrift stores like to keep the ones they get for their own use. New ones are very expensive. Sewing dummies can be used with a long dress to cover the missing limbs.

One old trick is to stuff long johns and sew the openings and "joints." The dotted lines indicate the points that will need to be sewn closed.

The biggest problem with this method is the flexible limbs. Parts of the body bend where they should not. If you stick 1" × 2" wood studs into the limbs before sewing the long johns shut, the body will keep a realistic shape.

A simple wooden skeleton can be made by hinging the studs together with nylon cord. Then wrap the "bones" with foam and duct tape. Cover this "skeleton" with old clothing.

Heads for these dummies are described on the next page. Hands can be bought from novelty shops, as can skeleton hands and heads. If you dress your wooden skeleton in clothing *without* wrapping the wood studs in foam, then attach skeleton hands and heads, you'll have a convincing full skeleton.

Getting a Head

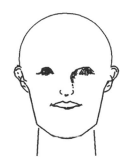

Buy this Styrofoam wig holder from a wig shop. The male version costs about $15. (Complete female rubber heads can be bought from a barber or cosmetology school for about $18. These will have hair and be painted to look somewhat real.)

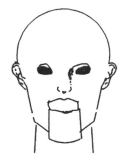

Cut the mouth on the Styrofoam head so that it can be pulled open a little. Cut out sockets for the eyes. Punch holes for the nostrils.

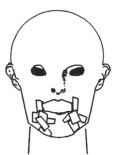

Carve the chin down and tape the sides of the mouth with white duct tape. Carefully paint the inside of the mouth and eye sockets red or dark pink. Seal the entire head by spray-painting it with a base coat of flesh-colored paint. After it is dry, coat with many thin layers of flesh-tinted natural latex.

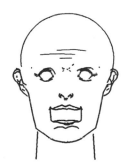

Lightly paint black flesh lines and add red to the lips. Let dry, then cover with another coat of flesh-tinted latex to soften the painted lines.

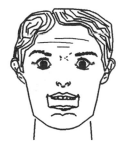

Pop in a pair of fake eyeballs and glue on a wig. Buy a cheap set of vampire fangs and trim off the long fangs. This will leave a plastic set of normal-looking teeth. Paint red gums at the base of the teeth and glue them into the mouth. Glue a few layers of hair shavings (from the wig) to the forehead for eyebrows.

Eyeball Appetizer

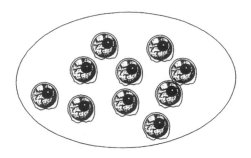

This delicious cold dish of eyeballs will add a disgusting touch to any zombie dinner table. These props can be bought from novelty shops but they are either too expensive or too unrealistic to be worth even the cheaper price.

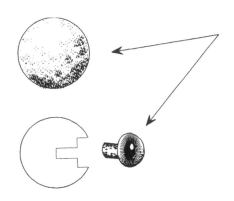

Buy round wood balls from a craft store. From the same craft store you can buy doll eyes, little plastic irises used for doll making. Get the brown ones as they result in a more realistic look. Drill out a cavity in each ball to accommodate the plastic doll eye.

Paint the ball white. When the paint is dry, use a felt-tip pen or a fine brush to draw red veins.

Glue the plastic doll eye into the ball.

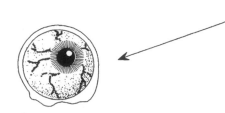

Place the eyeball on a plate and cover the eye with a thick skin of super-clear hot glue. If you cannot find the extra clear hot glue, use flex-glue or Climacel caulking sealant. Allow the excess to drip to the plate. When the balls are dry, pour a little red latex into the plate, or a little fake blood.

Base Frames

Many large props can be replicated by light frames. For example, a fake fireplace can be built from 1" × 2" pine. Always use glue to fasten wood to wood, even if other fasteners like screws or nails are also used. The exception would be for items that are intended to be disassembled.

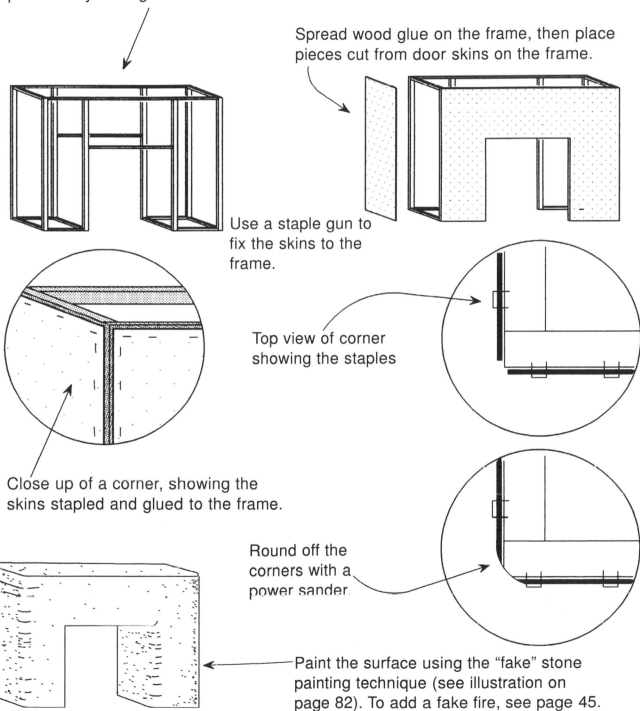

Spread wood glue on the frame, then place pieces cut from door skins on the frame.

Use a staple gun to fix the skins to the frame.

Top view of corner showing the staples

Close up of a corner, showing the skins stapled and glued to the frame.

Round off the corners with a power sander.

Paint the surface using the "fake" stone painting technique (see illustration on page 82). To add a fake fire, see page 45.

5. Costumes

Costumes add to the total effect. Total effect is the combination of acting, makeup, light and shadow, props, sound, stage or set, and costume.

Any haunted house operators who are not in costume should be dressed entirely in black from tip of toe to top of head. This is not just for ambiance. It creates the image of a uniform and helps to downplay the operators' presence. This is the same principle used by Japanese puppeteers, who dress all in black; although they are in plain sight while standing over their puppets to operate them, the audience focuses on the puppets and tunes out the puppeteer. I suggest black turtleneck long-sleeved shirts, black sweat pants or slacks, black socks, and black boots or loafers.

Most haunted house costumes can be found at the thrift store. Old suits and Victorian-style dresses are preferred. Capes and "T-tunic" robes (see illustration on page 94) are easily made. Check your library or local sewing supply store for books on costuming.

Here are some suggestions for home-made costumes:

Witch or Skeleton: Use a black choir robe or an old-style black dress. All exposed flesh should be covered with makeup.

Monster: Use old fur coats. Cut one to sew into pants. Or use shaggy fake fur from a cloth store. The fake fur is normally sold for stuffed animals. It is often too bright or too evenly colored (no variation of shade), but I have had much success at touching up craft fur with *light* coats of black and brown spray paint. Use pictures of animals as a reference. Use an airbrush if you can, but I have had good results with regular spray cans. For face and hands, see the section on makeup techniques.

Demon: Use an old jumpsuit and glue on foam shapes for unusual body features and protrusions. Cover the whole thing with a flex-glue or latex skin and spray paint. For face and hands, see page 108.

Zombie: An old thrift store suit that has been torn and spray-painted brown and black to look dirty. For face and hands, see page 110.

Remember to check thrift stores first!

Costumes don't necessarily have to be sewn; they can be glued, taped, or stapled with a regular stapler. Still, if you must rent professional costumes to preserve a realistic total effect, *do it!* The money will be well spent.

The T-Tunic

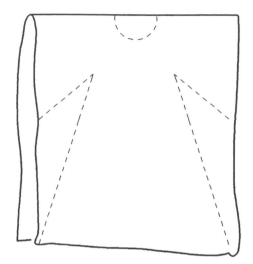

Fold several yards of fabric in half and cut along the dotted line as shown in the drawing.

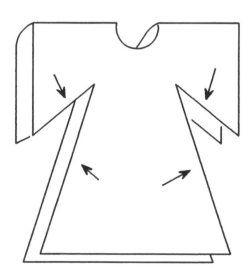

Sew the seams where indicated by the arrows. Then turn the garment inside out to complete the costume.

Latex Mask Making

Although buying rubber masks will probably be your first option, sometimes a particular character cannot be found at the costume shops. Also, you may prefer to avoid the "big head" look of most store-bought masks, which are oversized for a one-size-fits-all approach. The result can look comical instead of scary. Given these problems with commercial masks, you may want to consider casting your own.

One of the basic skills of the special effects technician is casting from plaster molds made from clay sculptures. Learning this skill opens many avenues for creating medium- and small-sized objects that cannot be adequately made by refabrication.

It is not my intent to teach you clay sculpting, although I will provide some tips that apply to this particular use of sculpture. I will be describing the process of making a plaster mold from the clay sculpture and casting a liquid latex mask from this mold. I am assuming that you will have someone connected with your project who is artistic enough or has been trained in the art of sculpting. If not, don't be afraid to obtain some books on the subject and learn to sculpt. This is how I learned. I was quite impressed at how well my first attempt came out.

You will need to be able to think in three dimensions, although the half-mask that will be described is not nearly as hard to work with as a full head mask. The full head mask would cover your whole head like a hood. The half-mask will just cover your face, although you can easily attach a long-hair wig to the half-mask and make it a full head mask.

Sculpting Tips

1. Sculpt the clay on a flat wood board (about 2' × 2') that has been covered with polyethylene plastic, so that when you are in the mold making stage the plaster will not stick to the board. Sculpt your image face-up (as though the creature were lying on its back).

2. Work from photos and drawings.

3. Do not use long or thin features on your sculpture. Such features are difficult to cast and are easily deformed in handling.

4. Keep anatomy in mind: bone anatomy covered by muscle anatomy covered by skin anatomy. Reference books on human and animal anatomy will be helpful. Some sculptors will actually build a bone structure, then cover it with a muscle system, then roll clay flat with a rolling pin to make skin and cover the muscles. This creates a great deal of realism as the bones and muscles shape the clay skin.

5. Most creatures as well as fantasy monsters are bilaterally symmetrical, which means the eyes, ears, nose, etc., are mirrored from one side to the other. This symmetry can be difficult to duplicate. Try putting a mirror on one side of the sculpture. This will give you a reverse image from which to work.

6. Leave all detailing and texturing for the last step. Don't try to finish one section of the sculpture and then move on to another. Each step should be part of a progression, from roughing in all the features to detailing all of the features.

7. Try to avoid deep grooves, especially around the eyes and in between the teeth. These can create extreme undercuts that could be difficult to work with even when

casting flexible latex. Undercuts are bottleneck areas that do not allow a hard material to unlock and separate. However, flexible casting material will pull from moderate hooks, curves, and bottlenecks.

Making the Mold

The mold is cast on top of the sculpture. Once the plaster has hardened, the clay is scooped, peeled and washed out of the plaster mold. You only get one chance at this. If a mistake is made at this point you will have to start from the beginning and sculpt a new piece.

You will need the following materials:

1. Plastic buckets, one for washing, one to mix plaster.

2. Casting plaster, molding plaster (normally used for wall patching), #1 pottery plaster, Hydrocal, or Ultracal 30. Any of these will work and all can be bought at a construction supply yard. The professionals use Ultracal 30, which is considered the best for casting fine details. Plaster is a flourlike powder that is mixed with water. You will need about 10 to 20 pounds of plaster for the mold.

3. Burlap cut into strips about 6" long by 2" to 3" wide. You will need about 15 to 30 strips. Medical cloth gauze or some other thick cotton material will work. It needs to have a large weave pattern to soak up wet plaster.

4. Plaster rasp.

5. Rubber spatula.

6. Small and medium-sized disposable camel-hair paintbrushes.

A few comments on using plaster: First, *never pour plaster or plaster water down a*

drain. It will harden and stop up the pipes. Instead, set the bucket of mixed plaster aside. The plaster in the water will settle to the bottom of the bucket in a day or so. Break up the leftover plaster and throw it away. The plaster water can be poured into empty milk bottles and thrown away. This is not an environmentally hazardous material.

When mixing plaster, always put the water in the bucket first, and then add the plaster. Remember, powder is always added to liquid.

The plaster will set faster with warm water and slower with cold. Use cold water for the first splash coat of plaster. A little vinegar will chemically slow the drying time, and salt will speed the drying time. But don't use these additives unless necessary. The exact amount depends on circumstances, and it will take experimenting to determine the proper quantities. Never use stored plaster without mixing a test batch, as it can absorb moisture from the air.

The plaster will heat up as it dries and can get very hot in large quantities, so be careful. *Never try to cast a body part such as your hands in plaster.* People have had their fingers burned off when the plaster became too hard to pull free and the heat slowly cooked their digits.

When you are ready to begin your mold making procedure, set up one bucket of warm water to be used for washing only. Have cold water and your empty mixing bucket on hand. Now follow these steps:

1. Put about four cups of cold water into the mix bucket. Sift plaster into the water until a soggy paste (similar to pancake batter) has developed. Mix with your hands until all of the lumps are smoothed and the paste is creamy.

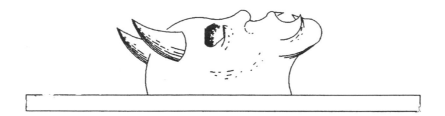

This is a monster half-head sculpted in clay. It rests on a flat wood board (about 2' × 2'). If the clay is water-based you must make the mold before the clay dries, because as it dries the sculpture will crack. You can lay wet towels onto the piece and spray it with a water mister to keep it wet until you are ready to make the mold.

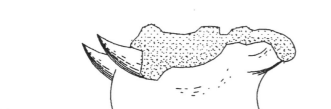

Brush the splashcoat on with a brush. Blow out any bubbles that may get trapped in the plaster. Use short blasts of air or a large needle.

The splashcoat must cover the sculpture with a layer about ¼" thick.

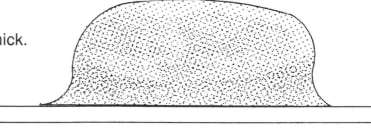

(continued on next page)

Once the splashcoat has almost dried, apply a layer of plaster-soaked strips of fabric. Press out any trapped air. Apply a second layer. Smooth each piece carefully down to the hard plaster.

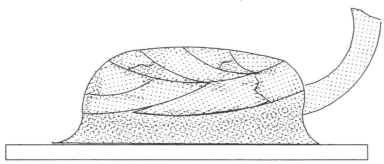

After the cloth and plaster have covered the splashcoat, cover them with the remaining plaster to create the top coat. Spread it over the piece evenly with a rubber spatula.

Once the plaster had dried, use a rasp to flatten the top. Be careful not to go too deep. This will serve as a bottom for the mold to sit on for the rubber casting process.

2. Apply this plaster "batter" to the sculpture. Starting from the lower areas, work up to the top to avoid trapping air bubbles. If the piece does not have many depressions along the sides, you may start from the top and work down. Any little bubbles can be worked out by sharp blasts of air from your mouth.

3. Pour the remaining plaster onto the sculpture. The plaster will heat up and dry in minutes, so work quickly.

4. Rinse the mix bucket, remembering not to pour plaster down the drain. Refill with 12 cups of warm water. Mix the plaster as in step 1, but make the consistency somewhat thinner. You will be soaking the cloth strips in this and applying them to the sculpture as if you were wrapping a broken arm in a plaster cast. Just soak the strips, lightly squeeze out some of the plaster-water, and smooth the strips on, as you would for papier-mâché. The strips must be loaded with plaster, which must be neither too watery (it will be too weak) nor too dry (it will not stick). Be sure to press out any trapped air. Build two layers of cloth strips.

5. After the cloth has been applied, sift in more plaster to thicken the remaining mix. Spread this paste onto the cloth strips to create a plaster shell, and smooth it with the spatula to spread it evenly. Once it has dried, use a rasp to create a flat spot on top. (This will be used as a bottom for the mold.) Be careful not to go too deep. As the mold sets it will get very hot. Wait a full day for the mold to cool.

Casting Procedure

You will need the following materials:

1. Ammonia-based latex rubber. You will need about two gallons. You can get it from a special effects distributor, a chemical supply house or a sculpting supply house. Be sure you do not buy the water-based latex. Water-based is used for skin application of prosthetics. Unfortunately, sculpting supply houses are starting to carry only the water-based type because of government pressure to reduce hazardous material handling. Ammonia is not that dangerous; it can be bought as a household cleaning agent. But the government paints with a broad brush. (Even salad oil in large quantities must be handled by licensed personnel.)

2. Talcum powder. This is used to powder the inside of the mask before it is peeled from the mold to prevent the mask from sticking to itself, the same way that balloons and rubber gloves are powdered on the inside.

3. Hair dryer.

4. Liquid laundry detergent.

5. Rubbing alcohol.

6. Small camel-hair brushes.

With these materials assembled, follow the steps described below:

1. Remove all clay from the mold. Clean the mold with liquid laundry detergent and water. Use alcohol and small brushes to clean the detailed crevasses.

2. When the mold is clean, *but not dry*, brush in a thin coat of latex. This is to ensure accurate reproduction of the details. If your mask comes out with tiny holes, the plaster mold was too dry. Before casting you may need to dampen the plaster mold with water.

3. Pour the latex into the mold to fill it halfway. Rock the mold to agitate the liquid and release the trapped air.

4. Pour in more latex to fill the mold.

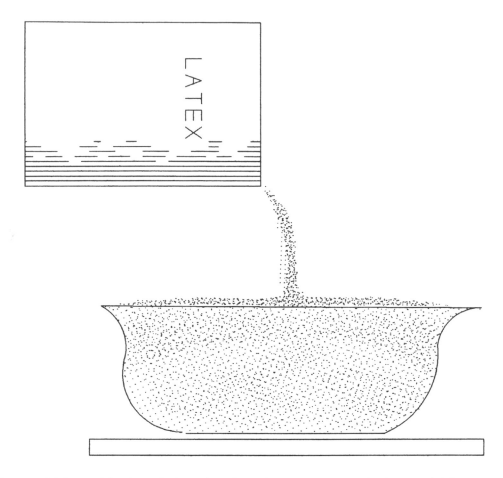

After the mold has dried and the clay has been removed, the mold is turned so that the cavity faces up. Pour liquid rubber latex into the cavity. Let this latex sit for 20 minutes to an hour. The dried plaster will absorb the ammonia from the latex and cause a thin skin to develop against the wall of the plaster. Pour the remaining liquid back into its container. Allow the latex skin inside the mold to dry. Repeat procedure as needed (up to five times) to develop a durable thickness.

5. Let the latex sit in the mold for 20 minutes to an hour. The exact time will vary with the type of plaster and latex used, so you will have to experiment. Don't worry if you don't get it right the first time. You can make many casts from this single mold.

6. Pour the latex from the mold back into the latex container. A thin coating will remain in the mold. Rotate the mold as you pour to leave an even coat. You may need help lifting and tipping a large mold. Be sure to strain out any lumps of hardened latex before closing the container.

7. Turn the mold upside-down for ten minutes to thoroughly drain.

8. Reposition the mold upright and use a hair dryer or fan to facilitate drying. Try not to super-heat the latex. Keep the dryer a foot or more from the latex.

9. For a durable thickness you may need to repeat steps 3 through 8 as many as five times. Let the latex sit overnight for the final step of casting.

10. When the latex mask is done, powder the inside and carefully peel it from the mold. At this point the mask is dried but not cured. Once the mask is out of the mold, it should be gently stuffed with plastic bags and allow to cure for a day. After it has cured, it can be washed with soap and water, then painted (see Surface Treatments and Finishes, pages 76–79).

Makeup Techniques

Many inexpensive makeup kits can be bought from costume and novelty stores. Most are fine for the amateur. A more professional kit can be bought from theatrical supply distributors. These are intended for actors in community and college theaters. A decent kit can be assembled by simply buying the individual components from various sources like drugstores or department stores.

Be sure to have the kits cleaned between performances. The containers and the top layer of makeup inside the containers will become messy. The next makeup session will become more difficult if the mess is not kept to a minimum, and the colors will get muddy from handling.

Your actors or designated makeup person should run a few practice sessions before the actual performances. This will give your team an idea of the time it will take and whether they have everything they need; and of course, applying horror makeup is a skill that needs to be practiced.

You should wash your skin and apply a roll-on or cream antiperspirant (even on your face) to keep from sweating the makeup off. Remember to use an antiperspirant only; you don't need the kind that is mixed with a deodorant.

All exposed flesh should match the face makeup. This includes the neck, arms and hands.

Two of the biggest mistakes amateurs make are applying too much makeup and not powdering the makeup after application. Powdering with a flesh-colored powder soaks up the oil in the makeup to lock the liquids and pastes. This will keep the makeup from smearing and correct the shiny effect of the oil. Do not use common talcum powder, which is bad for your lungs. Buy flesh- and white-tinted powder from cosmetic or theatrical supply houses. You can use cornstarch, but the effect is not as good. Lightly pat the powder on with a powder puff. Do not wipe it on. Very light strokes will knock off the excess powder, but hard wiping will smear the makeup.

Nontoxic, washable children's paint can be used with good-quality, extra-fine paintbrushes for detailed lines and dots.

Latex, Duo, flex-glue, spirit gum, or best of all prosthetic adhesive (such as Pros-aide) can be used to glue things to your skin. Duo is a glue made from latex and sold at drugstores for adhering false eyelashes. A good quality spirit gum is normally used for attaching toupees, but I dislike it. It dries with a wet look, it stays sticky, and poor-quality spirit gums do not stay stuck well.

Glue on prosthetics (fake body parts such as warts, a nose, scars, etc.) before putting on any other makeup. This will make them stay better and allow you to put makeup on them and your skin at the same time.

Warts can be made by dropping a skin glue onto a surface such as glass or a flat plate. Starting with the lightest colors, work your way to the darkest.

Remove makeup with mineral oil, cold cream, soap and rubbing alcohol.

The Simple Makeup Kit

Your complete kit should contain the following items:

1. Pale, dark and face powder.

2. Greasepaint sticks: red, black, green, blue, yellow, white, gray, brown and your skin color.

3. Red, black, white and brown eyebrow pencils.

4. "Scarstuff." Scarstuff is a very cheap wax with a cotton fiber filler. It used to be sold without the cotton filler and was much better without it. But it is still a good material for building small skin abnormalities like cuts, scars, holes, etc.

5. Brown and black crepe hair. Crepe

hair is fake hair that can be cut in small lengths and glued to the skin.

6. Makeup remover such as mineral oil, cold cream, soap and rubbing alcohol.

7. Black and red tooth enamel or wax. This stuff is spread on the teeth to create the illusion that they are bloody or missing.

8. Assorted brushes, tissue that matches your skin color, and latex sponge applicators.

9. Water-based paint: red, black, green, blue, yellow, white, gray, brown and your skin color.

10. A hand-held pencil sharpener.

11. Scissors.

12. Red, green, blue, yellow and brown food coloring.

13. "Super Polygrip" dental adhesive.

14. Latex, Duo, spirit gum and fingernail repair glue.

15. Fake fangs (cheap plastic ones can be modified to look okay; see page 106). Each actor should have his own.

16. Foundation: white, black and your skin color.

17. Fake fingernails (extra long).

The Deluxe Makeup Kit

1. Pale, dark and face powder.

2. Greasepaint sticks; red, black, green, blue, yellow, white, gray, brown, purple, orange and your skin color.

3. Red, black, green, blue, purple, yellow, white, gray, brown and orange eyebrow pencils.

4. Mortician's wax or derma wax, nose putty and "Scarstuff."

5. Brown, black, gray, red and blond crepe hair and long theatrical wigs.

6. Makeup remover such as mineral oil, cold cream, soap and rubbing alcohol.

7. Black and red tooth enamel or wax.

8. Assorted brushes, tissue that matches your skin color, and latex sponge applicators.

9. Water-based paint: red, black, purple, green, blue, yellow, white, gray, orange, brown and your skin color, plus glow-in-the-dark paint.

10. A hand-held pencil sharpener.

11. Foundation: white, black and your skin color.

12. Scissors.

13. Red, green, blue, yellow and brown food coloring.

14. "Super Polygrip" dental adhesive.

15. Red, black, green, blue, purple, yellow, brown and orange water-soluble pencils (these are sold at art supply stores for water-color art. I use the "Schwan All Stabilo" brand).

16. Latex, Duo, Pros-Aide, and fingernail repair glue.

17. Fake fingernails (extra long).

18. Fake fangs (cheap plastic ones can be modified to look okay — see page 106 — or you can buy the more expensive "caps" from a costume or novelty shop).

Special Makeup Supplies

There are many products that are made especially for horror makeup effects. Many of these are featured in stores at Halloween time. Contact a theatrical makeup supply house to check the prices against the local stores.

Bald caps: These rubber caps are used to create the appearance of a bald head.

Collodian: Apply this to the skin; as it dries it will shrivel up the skin to create fake scars. Sometimes sold as "Scar makeup" or "Burn makeup."

Colored hair spray: This is a temporary hair dye that is sprayed onto your own hair. Your deluxe makeup kit might include black, white, red, yellow and blue.

Foam latex appliances: Various rubber add-ons, such as bullet holes, character noses and chins, wounds and pointed ears.

Gelefects: This all-purpose makeup product is a gelatin at room temperature. When warmed it can be brushed and shaped on the skin to create wounds, pus and scars. No adhesives are necessary for application. It comes in three colors: blood, light beige and clear.

Stage blood: Stage blood can be bought at makeup and costume shops, but it is very easy to make gallons of your own. Many homemade blood recipes will include sugar or syrup to add "body." Avoid this stuff; it attracts pests and is hard to clean up. Instead, buy a large container of red water-based (tempera) poster paint and a small quantity of yellow and blue poster paint. Mix 30 parts red, 10 parts yellow and 1 part blue paint. If you want more body, slowly mix cornstarch into the paint until the desired thickness is achieved.

Wrinkle stipple: A latex formula to create old-age wrinkles on the face and hands.

Some Basic Makeup

Demon Horns

Mix flour, water, and white glue into a moldable mass. Mold the horns by hand and let them dry by baking them in an oven at a low temperature until they appear a little bit tan. Be careful not to burn them.

Attach the horns to your forehead with a skin glue. Roll little worms out of Scarstuff or nose putty. Press them against your forehead and the base of the horn.

Spread the outside edge of the worm onto the skin so as to blend the material with your forehead.

After both horns are in place, makeup can be applied (see page 108).

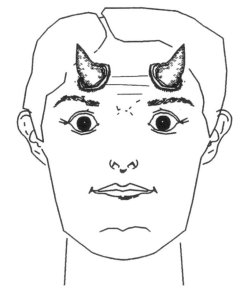

Shading and Wrinkles

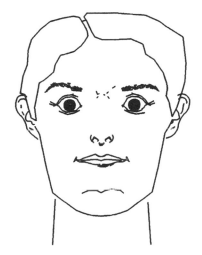

Sometimes you will need to shade an area of the skin to produce shadow effects. It is done by wiping a line of dark color across the target area, then smoothing the color outward from the center of the dark patch. Eye shadow or greasepaint is normally used to do this. The oil in the makeup makes it easy to smear.

Age or flesh lines are done in a similar way. The "wrinkle" is drawn in brown, then wiped in one sweep from the start to the end of the line.

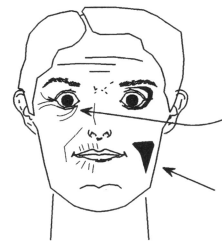

Draw the age lines following your own natural wrinkles, or scrunch up your face to make wrinkles and follow these.

Apply the dark patch makeup to the area that is to be shaded.

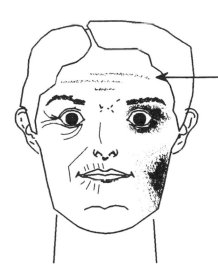

Soften the age lines by smearing along the path where each line was drawn.

Now smear the dark patches with sweeping rubs in an outward direction from the center of each patch.

Fangs

Novelty and costume shops sell variously priced "fangs." The best are "caps." These are two long, sharp teeth that fit over your tooth and are held in place with dental adhesive. These can range from $20 to $100. Simple, cheap plastic vampire teeth can be modified to look good for under a dollar.

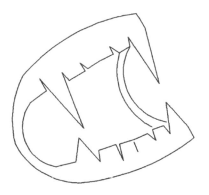

You will need Friendly Plastic. This is a sculptor's product from craft or art stores. It will melt in hot water and can be shaped with your hands.

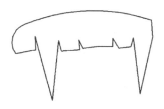

Cut off the bottom half of the plastic teeth and round off any sharp plastic edges. This will leave one large "cap" with a shallow cavity that will fit around the front upper teeth. Press warm Friendly Plastic into the cavity, then have the actor bite into it. This will create a form-fitting cavity.

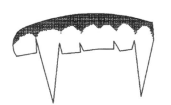

Using pink or red acrylic paint, create a gum line with several thin coats. Once the paint has dried, wet the cavity with warm water and pour in the dental adhesive. If you use paste instead of powdered dental adhesive you will not need to wet the cap first. Paste will fill better but may not hold as well. This depends on your particular set of teeth, so you may need to try both.

You can attach a similar set to your front bottom teeth for a different effect. Or use the bottom of the plastic fangs to create a canine effect. The bottom fangs are set wider apart from each other, unlike fangs that are used by bloodsuckers.

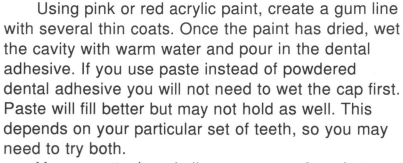

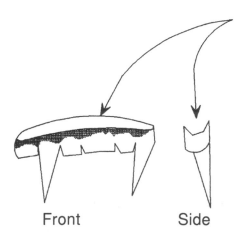

Front   Side

The Skullface

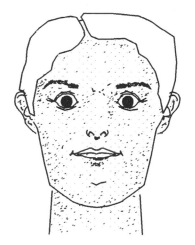

Prep your skin by washing and applying roll-on or cream antiperspirant to all surfaces that will be made up.

Brush the hair back and cover the skin with white makeup. Cover the eyebrows and lips with white makeup as well.

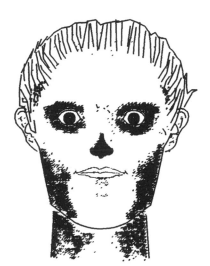

Draw a red line on the edge of each bottom lid as close to the eye as you can without poking your eye. This creates the illusion of bloodshot eyes. Completely black out the eyes and shade the temples, cheekbones and neck.

Black out the nose by drawing a triangle around it with a grease pencil and then filling it in with greasepaint.

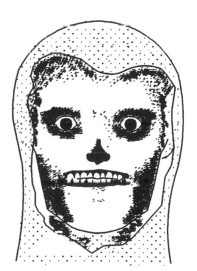

Cover the front teeth with the black-out wax. Put a few drops of blue, red, and green food coloring in the mouth to help black it out.

Draw teeth over your lips using black water-based paint and a fine brush. These teeth should go from one cheekbone to the other.

Dab the makeup with white powder, using a powder puff. Wear a hood to cover your hair.

The Demon

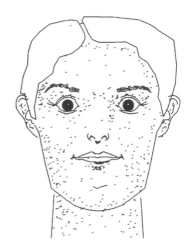

Prep your skin by washing and applying roll-on or cream antiperspirant to all surfaces that will be made up.

Brush the hair back and cover the skin with red makeup. Cover the outside tips of the eyebrows with red makeup as well.

With a black grease pencil draw a widow's peak where the hair come to a point on the forehead. When drawing hair use fine, short strokes.

Attach horns (see page 104).

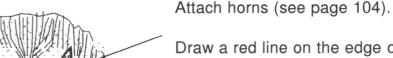

Draw a red line on the edge of each bottom lid as close to the eye as you can without poking your eye. This creates the illusion of bloodshot eyes.

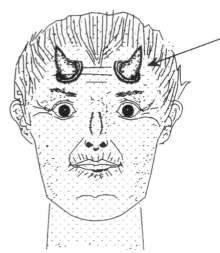

Draw flesh lines across the forehead, around the eyes and down the cheek from the nose toward the jaw. Draw light, soft lines on the nose.

Darken inside edges of the nostrils to make them look wider.

Darken the eyelids and around the eyes. The darkness should become gradually lighter at the edges. Draw dramatic eyebrows that taper up to the hairline.

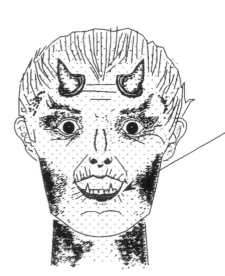

Put a few drops of red food coloring in the mouth and pop in the fangs over the *bottom* teeth. Color the lips green. Shade the cheekbones and the side of temples and neck.

Dab the makeup with white powder, using a powder puff.

The Vampire

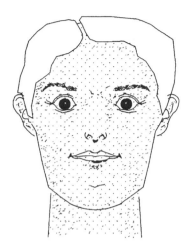

Prep your skin by washing and applying roll-on or cream antiperspirant to all surfaces that will be made up.

Brush the hair back and cover the skin with white makeup. Cover the outside tips of the eyebrows with white makeup as well.

With a black grease pencil draw a widow's peak where the hair comes to a point on the forehead. When drawing hair use fine, short strokes.

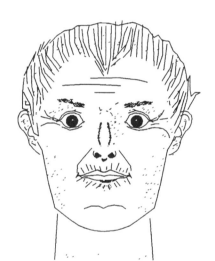

Draw a red line on the edge of each bottom lid as close to the eye as you can without poking your eye. This creates the illusion of bloodshot eyes.

Draw flesh lines across the forehead, around the eyes and down the cheek from the nose toward the jaw. Draw light, soft lines on the nose.

Darken inside edges of the nostrils to make them look wider.

Darken the eyelids and around the eyes. The darkness should become gradually lighter at the edges. Draw dramatic eyebrows that taper up to the hairline.

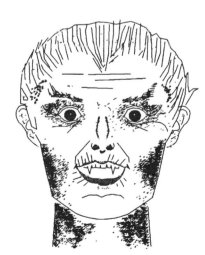

Put a few drops of red food coloring in the mouth and pop in the fangs over the top teeth. Color the lips blue.

Shade the cheekbones and the side of temples and neck.

Dab the makeup with white powder, using a powder puff.

The Zombie

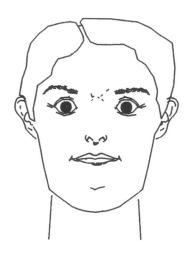

Prep your skin by washing and applying roll-on or cream antiperspirant to all surfaces that will be made up.

Darken the inside edges of the nostrils to make them look wider.

Darken the eyelids and the area around the eyes. The darkness should become gradually lighter at the edges.

Draw a red line on the edge of the bottom lid as close to the eye as you can without poking your eye. This creates the illusion of bloodshot eyes.

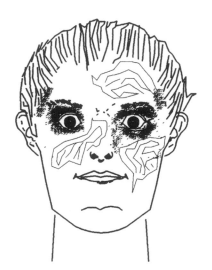

Apply tissue paper in patches as you would papier-mâché. Use cosmetic-grade latex or flesh-tinted flex-glue cut with water. (Do not use rubber cement.) Let the tissue wrinkle as you glue it on. Cover as much exposed skin as you can.

Coat the entire "mask" with a layer of the latex or glue to create a top skin. Use pale makeup on the top skin. Shade the cheekbones, temples and neck.

Use black-out wax on the teeth to create sharp and missing teeth.

Put a few drops of blue or yellow food coloring in the mouth. Shade the lips with purple coloring.

Dab the makeup with white powder, using a powder puff.

6. Sound, Lighting and Special Equipment

Sound Effects

One of the most neglected areas of the haunted house total effect is sound. If you have access to a college recording studio, generating the sound effects for your haunted house will be much easier. But even if you can't get fancy recording equipment, a little creativity and research will carry you a long way. (For inspiration and technical information, I suggest you obtain a book sold by Radio Shack called *Recording Great Audio* by Peter Utz, Radio Shack catalogue #62-10889.)

The cheapest route is to buy "canned" sound effects from a music store. Isolate the particular sound you want and dub it onto another tape. These canned sound-effect tapes will be copyrighted; technically, it is illegal to duplicate this material onto your own tapes, but unless you reproduce them for resale, you're not likely to find yourself in court.

I suggest that you use endless-loop tapes such as those used in answering machines. These are available in 10-second, 20-second, 30-second, and 3-minute durations. Be sure to get the kind that can be played in a normal cassette player. Remember when using these that they *cannot* be rewound and can be played only in one direction. If you try to rewind them, you will damage them. Once you've recorded your sound effect on these tapes, they will play continuously. You can also get continuous play from a normal tape in an auto-reverse player. (Don't put an endless-loop tape in an auto-reverse player!)

Either a three-minute endless-loop tape or the auto-reverse method is good for playing the house "theme music." The theme music is played as background sound throughout the house, and it helps to cover up the sound of electric motors and fans. Most haunted houses try to get away with clichéd organ or "funeral parlor" music for this purpose. Ask yourself, "Would I pay to hear this in a movie?" Most of the good horror movies use rock music or at least something with a hard-driving beat. Use an instrumental from a horror movie soundtrack. Do not use vocals as they are distracting.

Use a timer or a clock with a second hand when recording an endless-loop tape. Play the tape a few times and listen for the slight "pop" sound that will tell you when the end of the tape has passed the recording head of your player. Hit the pause button immediately, take the tape out and look at the bare magnetic tape of the cassette. You should be able to see the metal splice that connects the two ends. You can adjust the position of this splice by *advancing* the tape manually (don't rewind!). Use a screwdriver to turn the wheel gear. If you overshoot the metal splice or you are not sure, play it again. Once you have established the exact number of seconds your endless loop plays and you have lined up the splice of the tape with the head of the recorder, you are ready to make your recording.

If you use auto-reverse players and normal cassette tapes the quality of the sound will be much better. If you remove the "leader"—the section of tape that cannot be recorded on—you can record your sound effects right up to the point where the tape will stop and reverse. You can get cassette tapes that are held together by screws. The higher-quality tapes normally are built this way. Open the cassette. Snap the plastic wheel apart. Pull out the "leader" tape, cut if off, and reinsert the remaining tape into the wheel, then snap the wheel back together. If you cannot find a cassette built this way, you can carefully dab a little Super Glue onto the tape, and wind it back so that the top of the tape adheres to the bottom of the tape on the wheel. This will prevent the wheel from turning further once the tape has advanced to this point, so that the cassette player is tricked into sensing that the tape is finished. Of course you will have to record 30 minutes of sound on each side.

Sometimes you will want to tap into a recording so that the sound comes out of the speaker when you want it to, but is not heard when you don't need it. For example, perhaps you have an endless-loop tape of a woman screaming, but you only want to hear the screams at certain moments. You can tap into the tape for a moment by using electric relays or an electric switch. The wire that carries the sound to the

speaker goes through the switch or relay before being connected to the speaker. The relay or switch is tripped to turn on the sound.

When recording sound effects, try to buy the very best equipment you can afford. For playing sound effects, you may be able to use large sound systems bought from a thrift store. These will be powerful but inexpensive. Be sure to clean and demagnetize the heads of this equipment first. Kits for this purpose can be bought from music stores or electronic gadgetry stores. You can also clean the heads with cotton swabs and 100 percent isopropyl alcohol (grocery store isopropyl is 70 percent alcohol and 30 percent water, which may rust the heads). Demagnetizers range from $7 to $30; the one I suggest is sold by Radio Shack under the name Realistic and sells for $10.95. It has a small red light that tells you when it's done and looks like a cassette tape.

If you can afford it, buy several 14-watt portable stereo systems with detachable speakers for the various sound effects that will be played in a haunted house.

The best recording microphone for the least amount of money is a lightweight electric condenser microphone, which costs about $20. These are battery-powered, with a flatter frequency response than dynamic microphones, and tend to be directional. Because directional microphones have a greater sensitivity in one direction, they help to filter out background noise. (Omnidirectional mikes pick up sound from the whole room.) You must speak straight into a directional mike. When recording, place the microphone on some soft foam to help reduce vibration.

Home and semi-professional audio equipment uses inexpensive "unbalanced" lines made of a cable with two internal wires. The problem with unbalanced lines is that they tend to pick up interference. "Balanced" lines, with an extra wire for reducing interference, are more expensive. The longer the unbalanced lines, the more interference they pick up, so keep them to a maximum of 10 feet.

When recording, try to have all electrical devices in the building turned off, since motors and electronic equipment can produce interference through the electrical lines. An alternative is to use an AC in-line filter, which you can probably purchase for less than $15 at any electronics store.

To reduce unwanted echo, hang blankets on the walls of the recording room. The more soft objects in the room, the less sound will bounce around and the less "muddy" your recording will be; use rooms with plenty of carpeting, curtains, and soft furniture. Keep a proper distance from the mike to reduce mouth and lip noise.

Feedback occurs when the sound from your microphone comes out of a speaker and goes back into the mike. Monitor your sound with headphones so that the mike doesn't "hear" the sound. Some portable units cannot be used this way. One portable unit that can be monitored with headphones is the Sony CFS-1000. Other units have a feature that shuts off the headphones while recording. Do not buy this kind.

Automatic volume control electronically lowers and raises sound level without your supervision. For the amateur it can help to make the recording more clear.

Canned sound effects can be dubbed from one player to another using an inexpensive special adapter, sometimes called an "attenuator dubbing cord," that plugs into the headphone output of one and into the mike input of another. It uses a special resistor to equalize the impedance for good sound quality.

A cheap method for mixing sound effects is to use a Y-adapter or "splitter" (available from electronics stores), which will allow you to record from two players, from a player and a mike, or from two mikes. This way you can mix, say, eerie music with the screams of demons.

When recording from one player to another, don't just hit the stop button at the end of your sound effect. First turn the volume down to zero, or hit pause, or do both; then hit stop. This will prevent recording the crashing sound of the stop button. Use the pause button when starting a player as well.

Changing pitch can turn a woman's voice into a man's, and vice versa. An easy way to change pitch is to slow down the recorder, but this lengthens the words as well as the sound wave form and is thus unsatisfactory. Two devices that you may want to invest in are the electronic reverb control, which simulates echoes, and the electronic pitch control, which alters pitch. Practically, this is an excellent way to produce a demonic-sounding voice, a dog's bark, or the laughs from tiny gremlins. With imagination, you can even create thunder sounds using just your voice, a pitch control, and a reverb control. A reverb control can be purchased at Radio Shack for about $50. Note that a reverb control is not the same as an echo-and-delay device. Digital delay line and echo chambers produce effects that are often mistaken for reverberation. The echo effect is the repetition of a sound in its entirety. It is the sound that you hear at the edge of a canyon when you holler, "Hello," and hear "hello" back. Reverberation is the sound that you get when you holler into a steel drum or sing in the bath.

Some musicians' supply outlets sell devices called "pedal effects." These will add echo and pitch changes. Normally these are used with electric guitars, but with adapter plugs you can use them to record sound effects. They can cost between $30 and $100 apiece. There is software for computers with sound cards that will replicate these devices. If you have access to the Internet, get either "Cooledit" by David Johnston or "Gold-wave" by Chris S. Craig. There are others, but these are the two I like the best. Most of these programs run in Windows and use presets that will allow you to make simple mouse clicks to create complicated sound effects.

If your computer has a CD drive, a sound-effects CD can give you superior quality. Buy this CD from a music store. I strongly urge you to use a computer with one of these software programs. The software is free off the Internet and you will have all the tools you need for manipulating and recording sound effects.

There are also several $300–$1000 professional devices that produce digital sound effects, but these may be out of your scope and budget. A good one is the "MultiVerb" by Applied Research and Technology, Inc., 215 Tremont St., Rochester, New York 14608-2366, (716) 436-2720. It has all of the digital effects you would need for about $300.

Speakers

Impedance measures how much an input or output resists the signal traveling through it. The input of the amplifier must have an impedance that matches the source feeding it. The output of an amplifier also needs an impedance that matches the speaker attached to it. Most home speakers are 8 ohms and may have a label on the back reading, "8W." Thus, most stereo amplifiers for the home have 8 ohm speaker outputs. Some home stereo amplifiers have outputs for speakers with different impedance. Smaller speakers may be 4 ohms, and a few speakers may be found with 2 or 16 ohm impedance.

A 30-watt amplifier can put out 50 watts. It happens when you turn the volume way up, allowing the signal to distort and create a lot of high frequencies. So guess what happens when you connect a 30-watt speaker with a 30-watt amplifier? The two work fine together until someone cranks the volume up, blasting 50 watts into the speaker, most of it in the high frequencies. That's how you burn up a tweeter. It's best to have a big amplifier but run it low, so that you are always feeding clean sound to the speakers. But you may want to buy speakers that are rated for 50 percent more watts than your amplifier supposedly can make. Remember, when adjusting the volume of sound in your haunted house, that you can take only two hours at 100 decibels or four hours at 95 decibels before your ears will be damaged. Your customers won't be in for that long, but your staff will.

Adequate speakers may be bought separately from thrift stores. Sometimes they'll be broken beyond repair, but they are normally so much cheaper than new ones that it's worth buying several and tossing out the broken ones. Remember that even if the speaker looks bad, it may sound fine, and normally speakers are hidden or camouflaged in the haunted house by spray painting them black. (Be careful to cover the front of the speaker before painting so that paint does not clog the speaker.) When selecting speakers from the thrift store, use this rule of thumb: The more it weighs, the better quality it tends to be. I know this sounds suspicious, but it is generally true.

Before connecting or disconnecting speakers from an amplifier, make sure to turn it off. Some power amplifiers can be harmed by short circuits while you're hooking up wires. Although they make special speaker wire, inexpensive 20-gauge lamp cord, sometimes called "zip cord," will work fine. It's available in any hardware store and is cheaper by the spool. Try to avoid splicing wires together between your amplifier and speaker. Each splice point (where the two wires are twisted together) adds interference.

When connecting two or more speakers to the same player, remember that they must all be "in phase." This means that you should connect the positive terminal on the amplifier to the positive terminal on the speaker, and the negative to the negative. If the wires are switched (positive to negative) on one of the connections and not on the other speakers, one or more speakers will be moving forward while the others are moving back. The out-of-phase speakers will interfere with the others' sound waves, and the result will be very poor sound quality.

Lighting

It is not the intention of this book to provide a full education on electronics and electrical wiring, but you need good, solid information to construct and wire electrical equipment and lights. I suggest you obtain books on house AC wiring if you plan to do anything more than plug in an appliance or lamp. Most of the worst fires in haunted houses have been the result of faulty AC wiring.

Black Lights

Use only the highest quality black lights. There are many cheap brands and quasi-black lights sold at Halloween time. They produce too much light from the normal spectrum and may ruin effects that need the ultraviolet spectrum. The bulb-style black light (it screws into a normal socket) is one of the worst. Use only the fluorescent bar style. I suggest looking for a General Electric or Sylvania light bulb supplier in the phone book. Their lights are more expensive (about $30 dollars apiece) but well worth the money. I use the F15t8/blb UVA source with an integral-filter, 15-watt, 18" fluorescent bulb. These will fit into most desktop fluorescent lamps.

General Lighting

When special lights are not being used to produce an effect, you will need illumination for the customers to see their way. Try to make your lights consistent with the theme of your project.

Incandescent flicker bulbs (with a normal 1" screw base) that simulate candlelight are effective. Clamp-on style workman's lamps are useful and can be bought from hardware stores. These have normal sockets with a metal reflective dome to focus the light in one general direction. They have spring-loaded clamps that can be attached to a variety of protrusions.

Always keep aware of how all the light sources affect the illusions. For example, spillover light from lightning effects or sunlight from an outside door that opens temporarily can ruin various illusions. Try to catch these problems in the design and construction stages.

Always check to make sure your bulbs will not burn any close materials or props. Incandescent bulbs can become very hot, and that heat tends to travel upward.

When handling high-wattage light

bulbs (200 watts and up) try not to touch them with your bare hands. Even with clean hands the natural oils of the skin will contaminate the glass surface of a bulb. This will increase the temperature on the contaminated surface and lead to a shorter bulb life. In the worst cases the bulb can explode.

Whatever kind of lighting you choose, be sure to buy extra bulbs and have them on hand in case a bulb burns out in the middle of a performance.

Special Lighting Equipment

Instructions for the illusions described in this book include notes about the light sources needed. While professional light sources can be rented from a stage and lighting supply house, many special light configurations can also be duplicated with creativity instead of spending the great sums of money that these supply houses will want.

For example: You could spend $75 a week for the cheapest spotlight. But if you shop around at secondhand stores you can find slide projectors for as little as $10. (Even if the bulbs in these projectors are good, be sure to buy backup bulbs.) Use slides to produce different shapes and color "spots." I use special clear glass slides (obtain these from a photography supply house) and hand-paint them.

For color I use glass stains. Once the glass stain is dry, I paint the edges with acrylic black paint to create the desired spot shapes.

Many theatrical supply companies will provide free samples of their "gels." Gels are plastic sheets that are put in front of light sources to create the desired shades of color. The free sample kits are 2" × 1" rectangular sheets stacked in a package. They are too small for the professional equipment that

would normally be used, but they are perfect for slide projectors. For ease of use I just attach them to the front of the projector lens with a little duct tape.

Once I needed a laser beam for a particular effect. I could not afford the cost of a rental, so I bought a high-powered projector (500 watts) from a thrift store. I made a metal slide from a tin pie pan, then I punctured a small hole in the slide. For a total of $12 I owned my own "laser."

Strobe lights are very overused in most haunted houses. There are few effects with a strobe light that don't look like something from outer space. Lightning effects do not look right with a strobe. Lightning can be done with a repeating photographer's flash bulb or just a high-powered floodlight. Remember that the customers spend most of their time in low light, so any light that is a little more bright can appear intense enough for lightning.

I once used a high-brightness flashlight bulb connected to a sound-activated switch that I pulled from a "dancing soda can" toy. The microphone for the sound-activated switch was placed next to a speaker that was playing a thunder sound effect. Each time the thunder sound boomed from the speaker, the light would flash on. (See illustration on page 117.) This created a perfect thunder and lightning effect with a low DC-powered light bulb.

Other Effects Equipment

Fog Machines

Fog machines can produce billowing clouds of mist. This "smoke" can be used to create many professional-looking effects. It

Lightning Effect

This set-up will work great for lightning effects in areas that are dark. Remember that the eyes will adjust to the darkness and any light will look like lightning in contrast to the darkness. A 120 VAC bulb can be used with the relay instead (relay contacts can handle up to 1 amp), but the low-volt DC light is much safer. Most of the equipment can be found at an electronic gadgetry store such as Radio Shack.

2 D-size battery holders (6 volts). Use 2 separate power sources to avoid electrical spike interference.

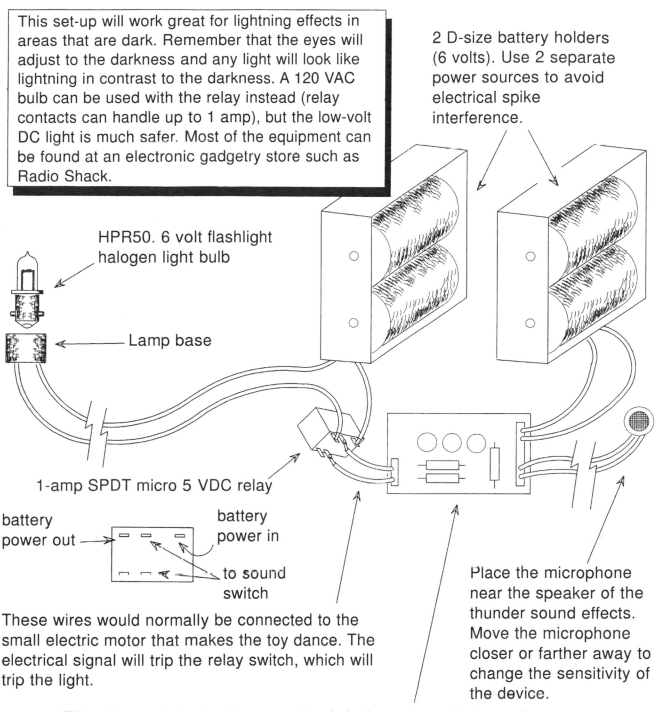

HPR50. 6 volt flashlight halogen light bulb

Lamp base

1-amp SPDT micro 5 VDC relay

battery power out

battery power in

to sound switch

These wires would normally be connected to the small electric motor that makes the toy dance. The electrical signal will trip the relay switch, which will trip the light.

Place the microphone near the speaker of the thunder sound effects. Move the microphone closer or farther away to change the sensitivity of the device.

This electronic device is a sound switch. It can be pulled out of a sound-activated "dancing" toy, such as the dancing cola can or dancing flower. These can be found at novelty stores or toy stores.

can illuminate a laser light beam (all laser beams require a smoke medium to be seen) or add to the effect of a fire illusion. And what graveyard scene would be complete without a mood-enhancing fog rolling by?

Fog units can be rented or bought from a theatrical supply company. I suggest using the smaller units. They are less expensive and produce more than enough fog for the average haunted house. If you limit your use of the machine to small bursts for each group of customers, you can probably get away with buying one gallon of "fog juice" for 30 hours of haunted house operation. Fog juice is the fuel used by the machine and costs about $30 a gallon.

You can also rent a device called a chiller unit that reduces the temperature of the fog, forcing it to hang low to the ground. Some people try to use dry ice for this low-fog effect. This can be more trouble than it is worth. In order to melt the dry ice, you must put it into water. The water tends to freeze up, so a method of warming the water must be used. The dry ice costs about $10 a pound, and one pound can be used up in less than an hour.

The fog machines can be rented for $100 or bought for $300.

A small fog effect can be produced by using a common humidifier. The best results are obtained with the ultrasonic type, which produces a low-temperature, thick water mist that will last for hours on one gallon of water. I use the model number 690-100 made by the Sunbeam appliance company. It costs about $60. Use a wide, curved PVC plumber's pipe to redirect the output of the humidifier. This cloud could billow out of a witch's cauldron or be used as smoke from a fake fire.

Air Compressors

Some effects can be automated by using air compressors and bicycle pumps. I automated a graveyard by sticking fake heads on the handles of bicycle pumps. I removed the one-way valve on each bike pump. Then, from each pump, I attached an air hose with an electric valve to a compressed air tank. Finally I fixed the base of each bike pump to the floor behind a gravestone and dressed the pump with ripped clothing hanging off the head.

Each time a customer passed a gravestone, the operator pushed a button that triggered the air valves, forcing the handles to pop up, raising the heads. Once the air valves disengaged, the air would bleed out of the valves to lower the heads for the next attack.

If you use compressed air, try to keep the pressure around 25 PSI. More than that is wasteful and dangerous. Besides, low-pressure vinyl hose is less expensive than reinforced high-pressure hose.

The compressor for the tank should be set up as far away as possible. These machines make a lot of noise when they kick in. The air bleeds from a release hole in 3-way air valves only.

I use the MAC 3-way valve model #35A-AAA-DAAA-1BA, solenoid-controlled, with 110 volts. It handles pressure up to 120 PSI, costs about $15, and accepts ¼" diameter threaded pipes. Contact Clayton Controls, 2925 College Avenue, Costa Mesa California 92626, (714) 556-9446 or 1(800) 235-4411. Air hose, connectors, and adapters to attach the hose to the valves can be bought from hardware stores.

Cables

Cable control is one of the simplest and most-used systems in the special effects industry. Whenever you need to operate an articulated prop such as the jaw on a skull, cable control is the most reliable and easiest to conceal. The cable is either bike-brake cable or engine control flex cable, which can be obtained from a hobby shop that carries parts for radio-controlled cars, boats and airplanes. The cable is a flexible metal wire housed in an outer shell. The shell and the cable work together to pull the articulating prop. The system will consist of the cable, the prop, and the "pull," a device that is hand-operated. A simple bike brake can be used for the "pull," but it is just as easy to make one (see illustrations on pages 120 and 121).

It may be necessary to lubricate the inside of the cable housing with silicon spray. Use as injection straw, then be sure to clean the cable ends and the outside of the housing with alcohol before using glue or friction connectors.

This little device is called a Kwik Grip connector. It can be obtained from most hobby shops that carry parts for radio-controlled cars, boats and airplanes.

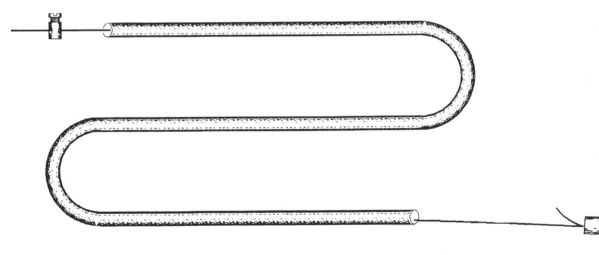

This small metal tube accepts the cable through its core; then it is crimped to grip the cable securely for various fastening and connecting applications. These metal sleeves can be bought in a fishing supply, hobby or hardware store. Use pliers or a hammer to squash the sleeve tightly to the cable.

Trigger Cable Pull

This pull will work for most light-duty work (short cables with rubber or low-compression springs). The device is held like a gun. The trigger finger is used to pull the loop. The loop is made with a small section of the cable housing to prevent the cable from biting into the flesh.

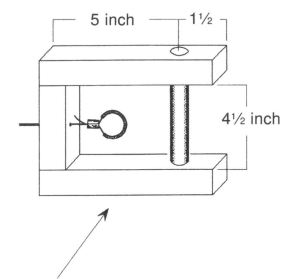

The device is made from 1" × 2" pine studs. Glue and nail them as shown. The dimensions will vary but are given here as a rough estimation.

The metal sleeve is crimped to form the loop of the trigger.

Drill a hole that will accommodate the cable but is smaller than the cable housing. Then, partway through, enlarge the hole to the diameter of the cable housing.

Drill a ¾" hole and glue in place a ¾" wood dowel.

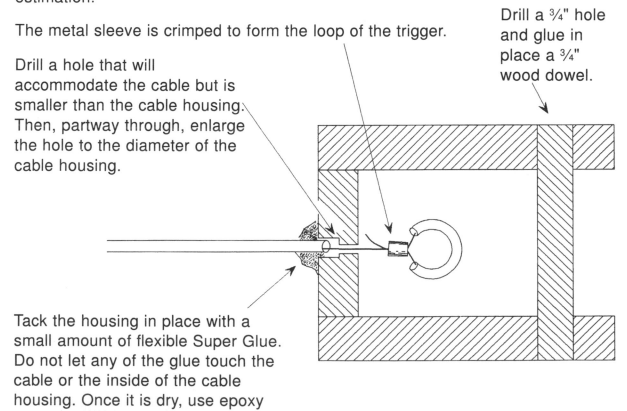

Tack the housing in place with a small amount of flexible Super Glue. Do not let any of the glue touch the cable or the inside of the cable housing. Once it is dry, use epoxy paste to make a more permanent connection.

Lever Cable Pull

This pull will work for most heavy-duty work. If the cable must operate against strong resistance (such as a cable length of over 3 feet) you may need to use bike-brake cable, sold in bicycle shops.

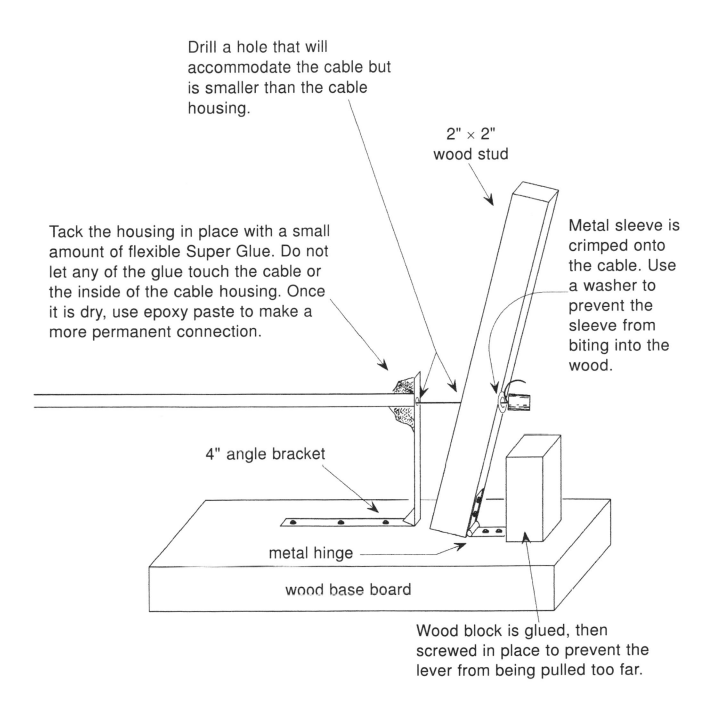

Drill a hole that will accommodate the cable but is smaller than the cable housing.

2" × 2" wood stud

Tack the housing in place with a small amount of flexible Super Glue. Do not let any of the glue touch the cable or the inside of the cable housing. Once it is dry, use epoxy paste to make a more permanent connection.

Metal sleeve is crimped onto the cable. Use a washer to prevent the sleeve from biting into the wood.

4" angle bracket

metal hinge

wood base board

Wood block is glued, then screwed in place to prevent the lever from being pulled too far.

The Talking Skull

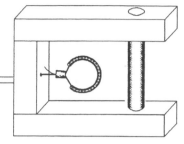

This skull is a plastic model that can be bought at most toy or hobby stores. It is life-sized and looks great.

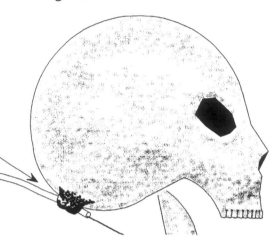

Tack with flexible Super Glue, then use an epoxy paste to make a more permanent connection.

This is an example of how the cable control can be used. The skull can be set up anywhere, and the jaw will be opened and closed by an operator hidden behind a wall or curtain.

The model includes elastic bands to keep the jaw shut. The cable pull will open the mouth.

You must drill two holes on the inside of the plastic jaw. These holes will not penetrate all the way to the outside. Cut a brass or steel rod long enough to snap into the two holes. This rod, about 3/32" in diameter, can be bought at hobby shops and hardware stores. Use flexible Super Glue to attach the rod permanently.

7. Advertising

This is the most critical area of a successful haunted house. Even if you created a terrible attraction with every possible cliché and dreadful "boo" technology, you could still make a lot of money with the right kind of advertising.

There was a bad haunted house produced by a big sponsor. The people they hired to design the house had no background for it. This sponsor was a world-famous beer company. The company hired a high school kid who was a good makeup artist but had no clue about the esoteric knowledge and demands of a first-rate haunted house. The results were terrible. Thousands of dollars of start-up money resulted in good background sets, but no showmanship. The house used uninspired, off-the-shelf special effects, amateur actors, and no continuity or theme. The customers were led from one set to another like cattle. There was no control of the volunteers, leading to a breakdown of the total effect. As the volunteers became bored, they would improvise with stunts intended more to entertain themselves than to please the customers. The egress was bad, with three-foot ceilings at some points, and the stairs were not illuminated. In a nutshell, it made me laugh and cry at the same time. This was not just my opinion. Many of the magicians, special effects technicians and the one other haunted house designer in the area agreed with my assessment. But you know what? The house still made more money than any other haunted house in the area, because the sponsor provided quality advertisement and a hell of a lot of it! Television, radio, billboards, everything; the beer company knew nothing about haunted houses, but they sure knew advertising!

You should spend at least 25 cents for advertising for each person you plan to attract to your haunted house; $1 per person for large events. So if you need 1000 people to come to your haunted house, you should spend $250 on advertising. But you can also get free advertising from television and radio public service announcements (PSAs). And, as always, creativity can reduce costs. You could, for instance, paint signs on 4' × 8' plywood sheets. Use 2" × 4" studs and drywall screws to make a sturdy brace and strap your signs into the back of a pickup truck. Now you have your own traveling billboard for very little cost.

The major categories of advertising are media such as TV, radio and newspapers, publicity stunts, and postings such as billboards, posters and flyers.

Media

Many local radio stations announce community events. Prepare a public service announcement (PSA) to be sent to radio stations. Ask that it be read during the "community calendar" segment. When writing a PSA, answer all the whats, whens, wheres, hows and whys. Keep it simple but complete. The average number of words you can say in a 30-second spot is 45.

Here is a sample PSA for radio:

Writer: Jerry Chavez
Date: Sept. 5, 1996
To be aired: Oct. 15–31
Time: 30 seconds
Public Service Announcement

(*Music and sound effects under.*)
(*Wolf howling.*) Have traditional haunted houses bored you to death? Then try some serious Halloween entertainment. The House of Nightmares features professional-style special effects and psychologically crafted frights that will scare the **YELL** out of you! (*Echo.*) The House of Nightmares is open from 7 P.M. to 11 P.M. from Oct. 15th to the 31st at the Westhaven Plaza in Fountain Valley. Take the 405 to Brookhurst Street across from Milesquare Park. For more information, call 714 555-YELL. Come to the House of Nightmares for Halloween excitement. We put the fun back into funeral! (*Screaming fades into echo.*)

Sometimes newspapers will do articles on local haunted houses and give a free mention of the locations, dates and times. Contact the newspaper and ask about an article. Even if they give you a free mention, you should consider buying a small advertisement.

A press release is a brief but complete description that informs newspapers of your project. When you submit this press release to a paper, a reporter will decide if the event is newsworthy enough to write a story. If you're lucky, that reporter will come to your haunted house to take pictures, but you should send a few black and white 8" × 10" or 5" × 7" photos with your press release. These must be actual prints on glossy paper. Be sure to provide the names of everyone in your photos. You should send a press release to all the newspapers in the area. Double-space the press release and type on only one side of the paper. Include your name and address and type "-30-" at the bottom of the page (this jargon indicates the end of the information).

Try to get an article, *plus* paid advertising, *plus* a mention in the paper's calendar of events. That way you would be mentioned in three different parts of the same newspaper. This is a good thing!

Here is a sample press release:

The Rainbow Coalition for Charity is presenting a Halloween Haunted House to raise money for the Flood Victims Relief Fund. The staff has gone all out this year to produce a professional-style attraction with illusions and scares rarely seen in most charitable haunted house events. 4000 hours of volunteer labor have been used to create the "House of Nightmares." The House of Nightmares will be open from 7 P.M. to 11 P.M. from Oct. 15th to the 31st at the Westhaven Plaza in Fountain Valley. Take the 405 to Brookhurst Street across from Milesquare Park. For more information call 714 555-YELL. Admission will be $8 per adult. This event is not suggested for small children as the effects are very realistic.
-30-

Publicity Stunts

Publicity stunts are intended to attract the attention of news reporters and to get people talking about your project.

Have some volunteers dress as monsters to tour schools, shopping malls and large factories at lunch time. They should carry flyers with them.

If you have a haunted house volunteer who can perform a few magic tricks he could give free demos in school classrooms and other gatherings, then pass out "discount" coupons for the haunted house. Normally, you must decide how much you will charge, add 20 to 30 percent, then give out plenty of "discount" coupons for 20 to 30 percent off. This is a standard marketing technique.

Sometimes it's worth giving out free tickets to children and young teenagers. Most of the time they will have to come with their parents, who may bring along more family members, all of whom will have to buy tickets.

You could run the haunted house one night for the handicapped. This could get you some free news time.

Postings

It is illegal in many cities to put flyers on cars, but being a novelty and a charity you might not have a problem. At least distribute flyers at fast-food stands and libraries. Some of the local merchants may allow you to post your flyer in their windows, especially if you have bought supplies from those merchants.

A sample flyer is on page 126.

Professional signs are expensive. It can cost about $180 just to make the die to turn out the signs. I could never see spending the $180 on just the set-up fee. So I used the money to make my own.

Design a large sign and divide it into halves or fourths. Have the segments photocopied onto 11" × 8½" orange-colored paper. Glue or tape them together onto cardboard. This can result in a large, professional-looking poster. Staple the poster to a 1" × 2" inch pine stick that's about two feet long. You can duct-tape these signs around town on street corners. You will need to go around later and collect them after the closing of the haunted house. Otherwise the city will do it for you and gladly charge your group.

You could try sending a cover letter with posters, memos, and discount coupons to large factories. Inform them that your event is for charity and ask them to post your information in the employees' lounge.

THE HOUSE OF NIGHTMARES HAUNTED HOUSE

Have traditional haunted houses bored you to death? Then try some serious Halloween entertainment. The House of Nightmares features professional-style special effects and psychologically crafted frights that will scare the YELL out of you! The House of Nightmares is open from 7 P.M. to 11 P.M. from Oct. 15 to 31st at the Westhaven Plaza in Fountain Valley. Take the 405 to Brookhurst Street across from Milesquare Park. For more information call 714 555-YELL. Come to the House of Nightmares for Halloween excitement: we put the fun back into funeral!

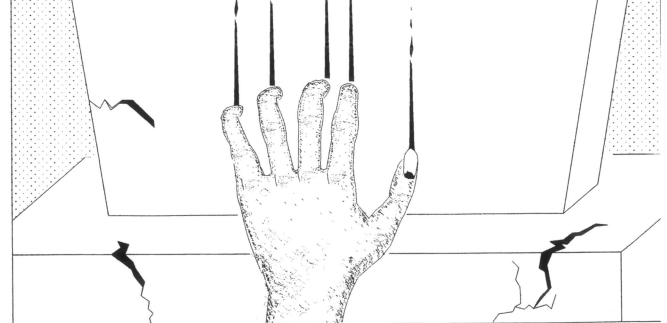

Last Words

As one of the main movers and shakers, you are going to be under a lot of stress sometimes.

I often find myself in a situation that at first seems hopeless. I once spent three months trying to locate some nylon tubing with a $\frac{1}{32}$" inside diameter. Every single source I contacted came up dry. I was told that it was a discontinued product. I knew somewhere in the world it had to exist. But every day I was told, "No, haven't seen stuff like that in years."

I thought about giving up on it several times. But I knew from past experience that the extra mile is a lonely stretch of road. Most others would have given up. Many of my successes have been achieved by not giving up until I was sure 99 percent of the population would.

I finally found that tubing at a plastic scrap yard, buried under some common rubber hose. It had a sticker on it that listed the date it had been sold to the scrap yard. That nylon tubing had been waiting under that pile of rubber for me since before I was born!

If you do what everyone else does you will not get any further than everyone else. Or, as a friend of mine more elegantly said, "No one ever got anywhere by being normal!"

Try to use your creativity (rather than money) to solve your problems. One method of jump-starting your creativity is to try to see the similarities between your problem and an elephant. I know this sounds wacky, but that's the point. By thinking this way your logical mind is confused into silence and your creative mind gets a carrot to lure it out of hiding.

I will leave you with this: It won't be easy, but don't give up. Good luck!

Appendix A: Checklist and Sample Timeline

The checklist below should prove helpful in organizing your volunteer workforce. It summarizes the jobs that need to be done to make your haunted house successful.

Item	*Description*
Bookkeeping and Accounting:	Estimate budget; put together a proposal to show investors; keep records of expenses and ticket sales.
Investment Capital:	Pitch the plan to a large sponsor or several small sponsors.
Location:	Find a suitable building or plot of land. *Don't forget parking!*
Construction Drawings:	Draw as much of the project as you possibly can. You will absolutely need a set of floor plans to submit to the fire marshal and to the city planning office. They must be submitted *several weeks before* any construction is started.
Building and Occupancy Permits:	After the city has approved your drawings, you will be issued a building permit and can begin construction. When the building inspector has passed your construction, you will be issued a certificate of occupancy, which the fire marshal may ask to see.
Fire Prevention:	Includes fire retardant, *heat* detectors (not smoke detectors), fire extinguishers, a panic light system, overhead sprinkler systems, etc.
Insurance (Basic Liability):	The fire marshal's paperwork may require an insurance carrier's name and policy number. You may have to purchase insurance, but most groups can use their existing policy for special events or buy a "rider."
Fire Marshal's Permit:	After the fire marshal has approved your drawings and your haunted house has passed an inspection, you will be issued this document.

Business Permit:	This permit helps the government get its share of your profits for taxes. Nonprofit groups may not need this.
Wall Materials:	You will need plywood, glue, drywall, drywall screws, 2" × 4" studs, metal drywall studs, and fire retardant paint.
Wall Construction Labor:	Depending on your local codes, you may use anyone who wants to help.
Electrical Wiring:	If you do anything more than plug in lights with extension cords, you will need a licensed electrician.
Decorations:	Obtain furniture and wall decorations that fit the chosen theme for your haunted house.
Props and Effects:	Once you have designed the house floor plans, you will need to "haunt" the house with spooky or frightening visuals and sounds.
Advertising:	The most important consideration! Plan to spend 10 percent of your ticket price multiplied by the number of customers you want to attract the haunted house.
Actors and Operators:	Best to have a surplus of help, especially if it's volunteer help. Unless you can pay them, you can't rely on all your helpers being available when you need them.
Security:	Off-duty police are the first choice. For a charity function you might get an officer for free. Otherwise it is worth it to hire them.

Sample Timeline

July 1st to 15th	• Research to estimate time and cost of all permits, plus the time and cost of all outside services such as fire extinguishers and insurance • Start prop and costume construction
July 16th to September 1st	• Start paperwork for insurance • Submit plans to city planning • Submit plans to fire marshal
September 2nd to 21st	• Secure plans and permit from city planning • Secure plans from fire marshal • Secure site with property manager • Start paperwork for utilities

	• Start production paperwork for advertisement
	• Set up account at bank
	• Start paperwork with accountant
	• Start paperwork for business permit
	• Buy wall materials
	• Start wall construction
September 22nd to 28th	• Finish wall construction
	• Obtain building inspection
	• Secure liability insurance
	• Secure business permit
	• Buy effects, equipment and materials
	• Buy props and decorations
September 29th to October 5th	• Start installation of effects and illusions
	• Start paperwork on fire extinguishers
October 6th to 12th	• Finish installation of effects and illusions
	• Secure fire extinguishers
	• Secure fire marshal's permit with inspection
October 13th to 17th	• Buy makeup and costumes
	• Hire and train staff
October 18th to 31st	• Performance
	• Start paperwork on dumpster for demolition
November 1st to 10th	• Strike (demolition and cleaning)

Appendix B:
Theatrical Supply Companies

Advanced Light & Sound Solutions
36 Sheldon Rd.
Manchester CT 06040-2319
(860) 643-8401

Angstrom Stage Lighting
837 N. Cahuenga Blvd.
Los Angeles CA 90038-3703
(213) 462-5923

Atlantic Stage Lighting
2900 Whittington Ave.
Baltimore MD 21230-1420
(410) 525-2525

Baltimore Stage Lighting, Inc.
1016 Azar Court
Baltimore MD 21227
(410) 242-3322

Bay Stage Lighting Co., Inc.
310 S. MacDill Ave.
Tampa FL 33609-3142
(813) 879-1513

Beacon Stage Lighting, Inc.
Market Industrial Pk.
Wappingers Falls NY 12590
(914) 297-1415

Bradfield Stage Lighting
209 3rd Ave. S.
Nashville TN 37201-2201
(615) 256-0977

Brent Theatrical Lighting
12 Whippoorwill Rd.
Springfield IL 62707-9246
(217) 546-9608

Brent Theatrical Lighting Co.
4048 Van Deren St.
New Berlin IL 62670-6751
(217) 483-4118

California Stage & Light, Inc.
3211 W. MacArthur Blvd.
Santa Ana CA 92704-6801
(714) 966-1852

Cannon Stage Lighting, Inc.
6707 Dogwood Rd.
Baltimore MD 21207-4148
(410) 298-0636

CCT Lighting, Inc.
1260 Lyell Ave.
Rochester NY 14606-2040
(716) 458-5790

Chicago Spotlight
1658 W. Carroll Ave.
Chicago IL 60612-2502
(312) 777-8824

Chico Stage Lighting Co.
100 Landmark Dr.
Chico CA 95973-9765
(916) 895-8233

CLS Custom Light & Sound
2506 Guess Rd.
Durham NC 27705-3307
(919) 286-0011

Creative Sound 'n' Light
5937 Haase Rd.
De Forest WI 53532-2976
(608) 242-1220

Damskov Theatrical Lighting
Fresno CA 93727
(209) 251-1424

DMF Stage Lighting
4505 Le Mans Way
Pensacola FL 32505-2619
(904) 438-8249

Downhome Productions Light & Sound
241A S. Union
Springfield MO 65802
(417) 864-5627

Dynamic Sound & Lighting
998 S. 2nd St.
San Jose CA 95112-5825
(408) 280-7488

Electralynn Light & Grip, Ltd.
4138 Shadyglade Ave.
Studio City CA 91604-1637
(818) 506-4692

Empire State Stage Lighting
18 Loralee Dr.
Albany NY 12205-2221
(518) 456-5254

Exciting Lighting & Sound Productions
1617 Fannin St.
Houston TX 77002-7647
(713) 650-1003

F & S Lighting Productions
Bayonne NJ 07002
(201) 823-4423

F & S Lighting Productions
174 Hobart Ave.
Bayonne NJ 07002-4359
(201) 823-9775

Fantasee Lighting
404 N. River St.
Ypsilanti MI 48198-2817
(313) 482-6565

Fitzgerald Lighting & Stage Rental
9308 James Rd.
Remsen NY 13438-3009
(315) 896-2785

Flashback Stage Lighting
1027 Greenfield Dr.
El Cajon CA 92021-3283
(619) 588-1048

Fort Worth Stage Lighting
2527 Weisenberger St.
Fort Worth TX 76107-1456
(817) 870-1591

Forte Lighting & Sound
162 Caddo Dr. #194
Abilene TX 79602-8043
(915) 698-6533

Galley Theatre Lighting
20 Aegean Dr. #16
Methuen MA 01844-1580
(508) 975-3498

Gemini Stage Lighting & Equipment
10218 Miller Rd.
Dallas TX 75238-1206
(214) 341-4822

Hals Stage Lighting, Inc.
10534 York Rd.
Cockeysville MD 21030-2347
(410) 391-8006

Hawaii Stage & Light Rental, Inc.
822 Mapunapuna St.
Honolulu HI 96819-2054
(808) 831-0333

In the Darc Lighting & Sound, Inc.
6425 Orange Dr.
Fort Lauderdale FL 33314-3339
(954) 584-2091

Innovative Sound & Lighting
San Francisco CA 94109
(415) 776-0234

Jacksonville Stage Lighting Co.
640 Lane Ave. N.
Jacksonville FL 32254-2823
(904) 781-6416

Jersey Theatrical Lighting
41 Veronica Ave.
Somerset NJ 08873-6800
(908) 846-4222

Kazz Stage Lighting
314 John St.
Rockford IL 61103-7025
(815) 965-5225

KB Audio Recording Service & Stage Lighting
2129 Roberts Rd.
Niagara Falls NY 14304-1897
(716) 297-3309

Knight Sound & Lighting Co.
9957 Darrow Park Dr.
Twinsburg, OH 44087
(216) 963-7760

L B Lights West, Inc.
2475 Maggio Cir.
Lodi CA 95240-8811
(209) 333-0996

Lighting & Production Equipment, Inc.
1700 Marietta Blvd. NW
Atlanta GA 30318-3647
(404) 352-0464

Lightworks Stage Productions
Naples FL 33999
(941) 353-6500

Luminescence Stage Lighting
1175 Park Center Dr.
Vista CA 92083-8303
(619) 598-8622

Lund Light & Sound
249 E. 4th Ave.
Escondido CA 92025-4901
(619) 489-8423

Maryland Stage Lighting
1 Rothschild Ct.
Gaithersburg MD 20878-4107
(301) 977-0151

Miami Stage Lighting
3149 John P. Curci Dr.
Hallandale FL 33009-3834
(954) 964-9016

Midway Stage Grip & Lighting
751 Park Dr.
Boca Raton FL 33487-3626
(407) 997-0021

Moonlight and Sound, Inc.
816 Donnington Dr.
Chesapeake VA 23322-7717
(804) 482-8636

Morgan Stage Lighting
2498 Southern Ave.
Memphis TN 38111-1528
(901) 324-4373

MSA Lighting & Sound
Columbia MO 65202
(573) 474-1327

Norcostco Stage & Studio Light
2089 Monroe Dr. NE
Atlanta GA 30324-4830
(404) 874-7511

Northern Sound & Light, Inc.
3190 McClure Ave.
Pittsburgh PA 15212-2366
(412) 766-8444

Oklahoma Audio & Stage Lighting Supply
2214 Research Park Blvd.
Norman OK 73069-8542
(405) 364-5733

Optasy Light Works, Inc.
316 Cello Cir.
Winter Springs FL 32708-3329
(407) 695-7524

Pacific Coast Stage Lighting
2446 Teagarden St.
San Leandro CA 94577-4336
(510) 352-2227

Parlights Stage Lighting
Frederick MD 21701
(301) 698-9242

Party PPL Light & Special Effects
Colts Neck NJ 07722
(908) 758-9555

Perfection Lighting & Sound, Inc.
740 Creek Trl.
Kennesaw GA 30144-2132
(770) 928-5900

Prism Theatrical Light
Union NJ 07083
(908) 687-5477

Prism Theatrical Lighting
1420 Seabury Ave.
Bronx NY 10461-3619
(718) 792-8162

Production Arts Lighting, Inc.
35 Oxford Dr.
Moonachie NJ 07074-1020
(201) 440-9224

Production Arts Lighting W, Inc.
10741 Sherman Way
Sun Valley CA 91352-5136
(818) 765-8983

Professional Stage Lighting
601 State St.
Baden PA 15005-1740
(412) 869-5060

Rich Scenery & Lighting
918 9th Ave.
Columbus GA 31901-2845
(706) 327-8020

Rodewald Sound & Lighting Co.
8214 N. University St.

Peoria IL 61615-1845
(309) 692-4222

S K Light Shows
6203 Devoe Rd.
Camillus NY 13031-8631
(315) 487-0388

San Diego Stage & Light Supply, Inc.
2030 El Cajon Blvd.
San Diego CA 92104-1093
(619) 299-2300

Stage Door Lighting & Display
9080 Activity Rd.
San Diego CA 92126-4456
(619) 586-1334

Stage Equipment and Light, Inc.
5910 Breckenridge Pky. #B
Tampa FL 33610-4236
(813) 626-8500

Stage It Concert Lighting, Inc.
Fort Worth TX 76112
(817) 654-4040

Stage Lighting Concepts
Box #25282
Fresno CA 93729-5282
(209) 433-1536

Stage Lighting Concepts Production Shop
3280 Edward Ave. #C
Santa Clara CA 95054-2307
(408) 988-0877

Stage Lighting Sound
1321 Eraste Landry Rd.
Lafayette LA 70506-1920
(318) 235-3486

Stagelight, Inc.
2310 Richton St.
Houston TX 77098-3225
(713) 942-0555

Stagelighters
533 Belleville St.
New Orleans LA 70114-1116
(504) 368-3737

Stageworks Lighting & Production
123 Seaboard Ave.
Raleigh NC 27604-1145
(919) 839-2288

Stl Concert Lighting & Staging
1200 Main St.
Asbury Park, NJ 07712-5941
(908) 774-2669

Tipton Sound & Lighting
950 S. White River Pky W
Indianapolis IN 46221-1336
(317) 631-2703

Todd Lighting & Sound
37490 Glenmoor Dr.
Fremont CA 94536-5732
(510) 745-7291

Travis Stage Lighting
Salisbury MD 21801
(410) 749-1295

Trucco Lighting & Sound
Hayward CA 94545
(510) 670-2834

Twilight Theatrical Light, Inc.
538 Clifton Ave.
Clifton NJ 07011-3230
(201) 472-4769

Universe Stage Lighting, Inc.
308 W 47th St.
New York NY 10036-3101
(212) 246-0598

Index